Stories from the Heart

New Directions in Therapeutic Intervention

A series edited by *Marti T. Loring*, The Center for Mental Health and Human Development, and The Emotional Abuse Institute, Atlanta, Georgia

---

Volume 1
The Enchanted Self
A Positive Therapy
Barbara Becker Holstein

Volume 2
Sexual Abuse in the Lives of Women Diagnosed with Serious Mental Illness
Edited by *Maxine Harris* with *Christine L. Landis*

Volume 3
Stories from the Heart
Case Studies of Emotional Abuse
Marti T. Loring

This book is part of a series. The publisher will accept continuation orders which may be cancelled at any time and which provide for automatic billing and shipping of each title in the series upon publication. Please write for details.

Stories from the Heart

Case Studies of Emotional Abuse

Marti Tamm Loring

The Center for Mental Health
and Human Development

and

The Emotional Abuse Institute

Atlanta, Georgia

harwood academic publishers
Australia • Canada • China • France • Germany • India • Japan •
Luxembourg • Malaysia • The Netherlands • Russia • Singapore •
Switzerland • Thailand • United Kingdom

 Printed in Singapore.

Amsteldijk 166
1st Floor
1079 LH Amsterdam
The Netherlands

British Library Cataloguing in Publication Data

Loring, Marti T.
Stories from the heart : case studies of emotional abuse. —
(New directions in therapeutic intervention ; v.3)
1. Psychological abuse — Case studies
I. Title
362.8′8

ISBN 90-5702-553-1

To

Donald A. Devis, With appreciation for
his ongoing caring

Esther F. Tamm, My mother and supporter

Emotional Abuse Victims, With my hope and
encouragement during their transformational
journey to become survivors involved
in life's connections

Therapists and Other Intervention Specialists,
Who help emotional abuse survivors

Contents

Introduction to the Series

New Directions in Therapeutic Intervention is designed as a vehicle for the expression of innovative visions in the area of therapeutic intervention. Individual titles will examine the needs of special client populations and describe creative helping strategies within a theoretical context. The editor's hopes are twofold: That this series will serve as a collection of well-defined maps to guide caring professionals in their helping journey, and that it will provide new ideas and a sense of hope for intervention with individuals who, isolated and in emotional pain, reach out for connection with others in their human family.

Preface

After careful consideration, I decided to name this book *Stories from the Heart: Case Studies of Emotional Abuse.* This title reflects the organization of *Case Studies.* There is a brief three-chapter introduction acquainting you with overt and covert emotional abuse, perspectives, and scope of emotional abuse.

Then you are whisked into the first case of Jen, as you attend a therapist's interview. In the next two chapters of Jen's three-part section, analysis and information about emotional abuse are presented in the humanistic tradition, followed by intervention strategies. Thus, the reader sees and feels the struggles, pain, and violence of emotional abuse.

Readers are introduced to each case through the victim's own voice. This introduction may take the form of a letter, therapy interview, play, and so on. In this way, the reader shares in the heartfelt experiences of each person. The opening chapter is followed by a second chapter focusing on theory, as well as an analysis of the specific case with generalization to the larger problem of emotional abuse. A third chapter includes strategies of intervention appropriate to each case.

This structure is in keeping with the experiential mode of leading with the heart, generalizing to the principle, and then applying information to the individual as a representative of the whole group. It is this organization that is the real spirit and identity of the book.

I hope that through reading this book you will join me as a champion in understanding and confronting emotional abuse. Together, we must remove the crushing destruction of the self so inherent in emotional abuse. This process must take place among friends, in therapy, at work, and on a larger policy level.

Acknowledgments

Thanks to Esther Tamm and Don Devis, who are wonderful supporters in my life. Special thanks for direction and encouragement from editor Kathleen O'Malley. I appreciate the caring of my colleagues, especially Claire Blackwell, Dr. Louise Bill, and Dr. Sandra Bloom. Thanks for so much help from Roger Smith, MS, EdS, with theory, references, and research. Also, many thanks to Pam Borden for encouragement and Leigh S. Builder, MS, for providing theoretical insight. Wonderful book team members, who read and commented on individual chapters, include coordinator Julia Newlin, Marchelle Cephas, Erika Tate, Louise Spiro, LMSW, Roger Smith, and Leigh Builder. I greatly appreciate their support and nurturing of the book. Thanks also to Madam Sharon Bowens and Patti Hart, consultants to the book team.

I deeply appreciate encouragement of colleagues: Wallace Burgess, Angela Roberts, Linda Schnall, Dr. Mary Ann Dutton, Julia Campbell, Charlie Corva, LCSW, Barbara Brewton, LCSW, Dr. Christine Courtois, Virginia Vaugn, MSW, Dr. Naviar Barker, and Dr. Guy Seymour. Also thanks for the ongoing support from my extended family and friends: Sydney Feuchtwanger, Jeannette and Jennings Stein, Ella Falk, Maxine Chapman, Sally Yandell, Dr. Betsy Garde, and Bill Kimbro.

I am particularly grateful to the animals whose presence eased the long hours of writing, especially Buffi — the blind cocker spaniel who sees with her heart — her brother Corki — the tennis ball catcher — and Ichabod — the squirrel who recovered from a car accident and visited the window sill of my writing area daily to get nuts and deliver his song.

Heather L. Gelles spent her spring break from Vassar helping with this book and many other tasks to give me time for finishing the first draft.

Heartfelt gratitude toward all the emotional abuse victims who have shared their trust and journey with me. And I am honored by the self-disclosure and attempts to help by emotional abusers who heard me identify their various abusive strategies.

The Stone Center, at Wellesley College, Massachusetts, writings about connections was valuable, especially the work of Dr. Judith Jordan and the focus on community involvement by Dr. Judy Herman. I appreciate the caring and skills of attorneys with whom I have worked to help emotionally abused women coerced into criminal behavior. The judges and juries who have integrated testimony about this type of family violence into their verdicts have been wonderful.

Special thanks to Jacqueline R. Johnson. She survived family violence and makes presentations to attorneys and victims, helping them to understand the terror of emotional abuse. My appreciation to the students and volunteers, like Sandy Dean, who have helped me in my work. Ongoing admiration for the research and therapy by Roger Smith, an expert in the area of emotionally abused men. The support of attorney Drew Findling and trial consultant Denise de La Rue has been invaluable. Volunteers, like Debbie White and Linda Schnall, have made possible our work at The Emotional Abuse Institute.

Introduction

This book includes case studies of emotional abuse victims who, with the help of intervention and support, moved onward through their journey toward becoming survivors. These cases are "composites" in order not to identify any one person.

Intervention, rather than therapy, is occasionally used as a descriptive term to encourage innovative thinking about a range of helping techniques. While many therapeutic techniques are applied in these interventions, family and community resources are also utilized with an emphasis on the reconnection process integral to moving from victim to survivor of emotional abuse.

Emotional abuse is a process that is so insidious, extensive, and pervasive that it includes the total range of emotional harm and devastation. For example, not only verbal abuse but nonverbal abuse as well can be powerful and hurtful to the victim. Connection is an important process where harm can occur. There are three essential areas of connection that are damaged in emotional abuse. Two of these areas involve the external bond between: 1) victim and abuser, and 2) victim and community. The third area is the victim's connection to her sense of self, identity, and personality qualities.

While victims in this book are referred to as "she" and "her," and abusers as "he" and "him," it is clear that some men are abused by other men and by women. This issue is dealt with in *Emotional Abuse* (Loring, 1994), where the emotional abuse of both women and men is examined. As in that work, this book contains the view that women are both emotionally abused and physically battered in epidemic proportions. Since the term "battering" is often used to designate physical abuse, this case study book uses "abuse" when describing the process of emotional harm caused by a pattern of covert (subtle) and overt (open) violence. And violence is seen as underlying emotional abuse. This includes a type of thinking in which rage and disregard for the needs of another translate into violent thoughts and actions, as opposed to expressing one's feelings of anger without accompanying degradation and criticism of the other. Thus, terms like "assault" are utilized to convey the experience of emotionally abused individuals.

Emotional abuse is viewed as occurring both conjointly with and independently from physical abuse. As a separate kind of violence, emotional abuse is shown to be as denigrating and debilitating as battering. Yet, unless it occurs in the presence of physical battering, emotional abuse — which has been identified by many as more painful than physical abuse (Walker, 1984) — is often overlooked by therapists and society as a whole.

Stories from the Heart: Case Studies of Emotional Abuse is meant to be a cry of alarm, a beckoning for help on behalf of both victims and perpetrators of emotional abuse. This call for awareness is rooted in concern about the desolation and desperation, the profound loneliness and despair in the lives of emotionally abused persons. The call extends to effective treatment and intervention for traumatized emotional abuse victims. They must be helped to find emotional safety:

> The essence of trauma is that a person's sense of safety in the world is seriously compromised. The provision of a safe environment is the most important aspect of the treatment of victims of trauma. The sense of safety must encompass physical, emotional, social, and moral levels of care. (Bloom, 1994, p. 13)

This book contains some terminology designed to convey the painful attachment and terrifying process involved in emotional abuse. For example, the term "disattachment" is used as a means of capturing the victim's emotional ripping and pulling away from the abusive process, to be attempted only after the victim has regained a sense of self. However, "detachment" is not utilized, since it has been adopted by many in the therapeutic community to describe a "co-dependent" person needing to become less dependent on another. Many people often do not clearly understand that a self cannot become separate when it is diminished or destroyed.

Further, victims of emotional abuse are portrayed as "embracing the abuse" process in that they cling to the very person from whom they are seeking warmth and connection, although the violence of abuse frequently disrupts that connection. The term "disconnection" is used to describe the painful loss of connection and resulting trauma and grief experienced by these victims. At no time is the term "clinging" meant to blame a victim who is reaching out in desperation to embrace a loved other. Rather, clinging is a natural outcome of trauma.

A person may feel traumatized after reading portions of this book. Perhaps he or she will be reminded of his or her own past. Or maybe the sadness of emotional abuse will become overwhelming. At any rate, somatic symptoms such as headaches or a pervasive sense of sadness while reading, along with possible intrusive thoughts and difficulty in concentrating, could be warnings to the reader. Perhaps discussion with a colleague or friend will facilitate further reading. The reader's interest and concern about emotional abuse are deeply appreciated.

Part I

Emotional Abuse: Destruction of the Self

Chapter One

Emotional Abuse Pattern: Overt and Covert Abuse

IN this chapter, the differences and similarities between overt and covert emotional abuse will be explored. In addition, the impact of each type of abuse will be examined.

Emotional abuse can be overt and clear. When one partner calls the other such names as "stupid," "crazy," and/or "inadequate" in a repetitive and ongoing manner, the pattern of emotional abuse is observable. And when a victim is threatened with murder or other significant harm, this is a clear manifestation of abuse.

However, a subtle and covert form of violence is more difficult to discern. A husband questions the abilities of his wife until she wonders whether she is able to properly raise the children or manage her own life. A boyfriend continuously interrupts his girlfriend, suggesting over and over that her feelings and ideas aren't important. A lesbian conveys to her partner that her feelings don't exist by ignoring them. One gay man in a couple feels increasingly depressed as a result of his lover's lying, withholding money, withdrawn and cold behavior and exposure to AIDS. A child's grades drop in school after his brother and father demean and exclude him over a period of time. In these examples of covert emotional abuse, the subtlety and disguised nature of the abuse distinguish it from overt forms of threats and criticism that are easier to identify.

Covert and overt emotional abuse can occur along with physical battering. Or they may be independent, maintaining a pattern of demeaning and humiliating treatment toward the traumatized victim (Loring, 1994).

Emotional abuse and trauma

A victim may not be aware of either the covert or overt emotional abuse. This lack of awareness makes the extent of this insidious process difficult for a victim or therapist to identify. In the context of this unacknowledged violence, there is a sense of losing one's self. The victim feels attacked and assaulted without understanding why. She begins to internalize the put-downs and demeaning treatment from the batterer, leading to profound sadness and decreased self-esteem. In fact, she loses touch with even those parts of herself that she has previously valued. The confusion and fear result in trauma and a sense of hopelessness. The despair derives from the victim's continual efforts to gain acceptance, approval and love from the abuser.

The Post-traumatic Stress Disorder is experienced by many emotionally abused women (American Psychiatric Association, 1994). This traumatic state is marked by confusion, flashbacks, intrusive thoughts, poor sleep, depression and a sense of hopelessness. For the emotional abuse victim, losing her sense of self results from emotional assaults and degradation. Like erosion of soil from the continuous flow of water, the self becomes eroded by on-going put-downs and criticism, discounting of feelings and ideas, and rage-filled yelling and belittling. Trauma results both from this erosion and from a striking episode of degradation/threats to emotional and physical well-being. This trauma is also caused by destruction of the self.

Destruction of the self

Destruction of the self involves such processes as self death (Niles, 1992) and disintegration (Niles, 1992). Niles (1992) described a process of metaphorical dying, which involves a disintegration of one's self. Following a trauma, the individual's feelings are split off from the experience and psychic numbness follows. The traumatized individual feels emotionally dead, devoid of feeling and sensory input. Rather, a deathlike sense of numbness and disintegration, lack of wholeness and sense of self leave the victim without an inner anchor- a sense of trust regarding her own perceptions and feelings.

In addition, Kohut (1986) depicted a fragmentation process in which an individual experiences 1) the loss of self, 2) estrangement from her body and 3) the temporary break-up of one's sense of time continuity. The victim loses the awareness of ownership and control over her body parts, which feel disjointed without a sense of connectedness. The victim also loses a sense of time in that she is preoccupied with attempts to understand the criticisms and discounts of the abuser. Moreover, the victim questions her own worth and even her right to form ideas and opinions. The resulting fragmentation of the self, stemming from a lack of empathy from the significant other, leads to difficulty in maintaining a sense of wholeness. The individual experiences a lack of cohesion. There is likely to be subsequent confusion regarding both the passage of time in the present and specific dates of historical occurrences in her life. Thus, many emotional abuse victims do not realize the actual time in the midst of preoccupation and flooding of negative labels or other criticisms.

Ochberg (1991) described a diminished sense of self that results from exposure to human cruelty and the feeling of dehumanization. Furthermore, Hammond (1989) affirms that emotional abuse causes a diminished sense of self. Sustained emotional and physical abuse harms at the level of the victim's sense of self, often resulting in feelings of inadequacy and incompetency (Hammond, 1989).

During the process of emotional abuse, the victim experiences shock and grief. Not only has the respect and warmth of another been lost during the abusive process, but many victims report a sense of disintegration in which the self "comes apart" (Loring, 1994). Many abuse victims describe not knowing who they are, forgetting their favorite qualities, experiencing an inability to think clearly and make decisions and feeling as if they are in pieces without being able to protect themselves. Thus, the trauma of emotional abuse causes this sense of "self-confusion" as if one's very being has been struck, attacked, assaulted and broken. This feeling of losing one's own integrated sense of self results in a struggle on the part of the victim to gain connection and affirmation from the abuser. However, the abuser reacts with additional overt and covert emotional abuse, further demeaning and denigrating the victim during her attempts to establish connection. This denigration involves shaming and belittling the victim. In the context of connection, the emotional abuse results in feelings of panic, abandonment, profound sadness and loneliness.

The overt pattern of emotional abuse

Emotional abuse is not an occasional put-down or criticism toward another person. Rather, it involves an on-going pattern of degradation and diminishment of the ideas, feelings, accomplishments and characteristics of the other. The underlying process is that of control and power. The abuse victim is not encouraged to grow and develop, since separation and individuation is threatening to the emotionally abusive partner.

Overt emotional abuse is clear and identifiable. It can involve criticisms and put-downs, like "You are so stupid and never do anything right." Threats to harm are direct when the batterer threatens to hit or kill the victim. In addition, threats to injure the victim's family, friends and/or pets may terrify a victim. This terror can also be caused by threats to abandon- to ignore, withdraw warmth and affection, or physically leave.

Mechanisms of overt emotional abuse

1) Threats: Life, physical harm, financial deprivation to victim or extended family (especially victim's children), pets, property, family, abandonment, institutionalization (accusations that the victim is crazy)
2) Financial manipulation
3) Yelling
4) Name-calling
5) Belittling
6) Accusations of being crazy
7) Interfering with job opportunities
8) Interfering with medical care through minimization, degradation (degradation of health needs), refusal to allow victim to seek health care, or attempts to control health care

9) Criticism
10) Sulking
11) Withholding affection
12) Ordering around
13) Monitoring time
14) Monitoring activities
15) Interfering with family relationships
16) Blaming victim for problems
17) Restricting use of resources: Car, telephone, etc.
18) Accusations of being purposefully hurtful
19) Jealous accusations
20) Restricting time with friends, family, special interests
21) Sleep deprivation
22) Emotional sexual abuse: Criticism of sexual performance, emotional coercion regarding specific sexual acts, withholding sexual activity, threats unless victim participates in sexual activities with animals; humiliation involving coerced observation of, participation in or hearing about third party sex involving the batterer and possibly the victim
23) Stalking

The pattern of covert emotional abuse

Covert emotional abuse is insidious, disguised and beyond the awareness of the victim. Sometimes it takes the form of questions, like "Do you ever understand about my feelings?" This is more an accusation than a question. The translation of intent would be, "You never understand my feelings." Or, a discount can involve an interruption of the victim's conversation, accompanied by the abuser's statement, "That's not important." Withholding affection is often subtle and covert. In addition, the abuser's walking toward a victim with his (abuser's) arms outstretched and hands in a choking position can be as threatening as a verbal threat to choke and kill. This body language of action mimicking choking is a covert threat to a victim who has actually experienced the choking and it is as terrifying as the actual act of being choked.

Covert abuse

1) Discount
2) Negation
3) Projection/accusation
4) Negative labeling
5) Abandonment
6) Denial

To discount another involves a pattern of subtly conveying the lack of importance, meaning, or value in the other's feelings and ideas. For example, continuous interruptions, along with suggestions that the contributions of the other are insignificant, contribute to the diminishment of self-esteem. On the other hand, negation is intended to establish the absolute lack of existence of another's feelings or ideas. The abuser may "speak for the victim" by saying, "You don't feel that way," when the victim has just expressed a feeling.

Projection involves the abuser accusing the victim of some feeling that actually exists only in the abuser. When an abusive partner feels inadequate, he may accuse the victim of expressing boredom or dissatisfaction with him.

In negative labeling, the victim is subtly labeled, as in an abuser's statement/question, "Do you really believe that kind of thing?" When said in a disgusted and demeaning tone of voice and continuously conveyed to a victim, this message covertly suggests that the victim is stupid, naive, or lacking in some other manner.

If abandonment is covertly threatened or actually acted out by the batterer, the victim feels frightened. This can involve subtle threats to leave the relationship or the abusive partner's ongoing emotional withdrawal from the victim.

When confronted by the victim, the abuser usually denies any aspect of covert violence. This results in the victim's confusion and depression.

Patterns of emotional abuse

Emotional abuse is not a one-time labeling of someone as "stupid" or any other negative label. Neither is it a rare and occasional put-down or criticism. Rather, emotional abuse is a patterned form of overt and covert violence that has as its aim the control of, power over and diminishment of another person's sense of self, behavior and thinking.

In the context of overt and covert emotional abuse, this violence is patterned both in the behaviors of the abuser and in the responses of the victim. Different abusers will manifest varied patterns of behavior. In fact, an abuser may demonstrate more than one pattern of abusive behavior that may be alternated. These patterns are threads of pain in a tapestry. For the victim, each pattern illustrates unique suffering and despair. For example, abusers usually engage in ritualistic emotional abuse that involves repetitive acts. These acts are usually present in a certain order during most abusive episodes.

In addition, many victims respond to emotional abuse in a patterned fashion, although they should never be blamed for desperate and traumatic responses to violence. Accident-prone behavior, despair, anxious-attachment, re-enactment of trauma, are all responses of emotional abuse victims. A closer look at these patterns of coping shows that victims are prone to have accidents while experiencing the trauma of emotional abuse, feel despair while re-experiencing trauma that is similar to one's past suffering, and experience anxious-attachment (Bowlby, 1988) where the traumatized victim clings to the batterer. Clinging during trauma is a recognized form of behavior in the field of trauma (van der Kolk, 1987). The tragedy of emotional abuse is that part of a victim's pattern involves clinging to the person she loves even while his emotional violence is escalating and her despair mounts.

The victim is often unaware of both overt and covert emotional abuse. Thus, the victim rarely identifies herself as emotionally abused when seeking therapeutic help.

Accident-prone behavior

Emotionally abused individuals often experience intrusive thoughts regarding the accusations and blaming words of the abusive partner. The emotional assaults wound the victim, who then goes over and over these accusations in an attempt to survive without loosing a sense of identity and self. While experiencing these intrusive thoughts, the victim's concentration is altered from *external awareness focus* to *internal awareness focus*. Internal contemplation of whether the accusations are true becomes the overwhelming concern. Thus, automobile and job-related accidents are common during these painful periods of *internal over-stimulation*. (Loring, 1994).

Furthermore, flashbacks occur after the emotional assault, especially when abandonment issues are involved. The victim's accident proneness is increased during periods of re-living the traumatic event.

Despair

Despair results from the anguish and terror of disconnection from the loved one- an emotionally abusive individual whose world view centers on his own discomfort, wishes and rage. The victim misses empathic connection in which another understands and sympathizes, encourages and honors feelings and ideas. The abuser is quick to criticize and demean, especially when he feels frustrated, inadequate, or threatened. Unaware of his own feelings, he perceives the victim as purposefully hurtful. His accusations follow and threats of abandonment are common. The victim feels profoundly alone, sad and desperate- all of which translate into despair. Her subsequent reaching out and clinging, in an effort to restore a connection with some warmth, is a consequence of despair and only results in further emotional abuse. Therein lies the fountain of her despair.

Anxious attachment

Bowlby (1988) described the anxious attachment of a child whose parent(s) are unavailable emotionally or physically for significant periods of time. For example, a depressed parent may be impatient, unattentive and lacking in warmth toward a child. Yet, the frightened child attempts to cling in an effort to obtain greater warmth, experiencing instead only anger and rejection. In later adult attachments, the victim re-enacts this pattern of relationship. This re-enactment leads to repeated episodes of desperation, sadness and profound loneliness haunting an emotional abuse victim.

Re-enactment of trauma

The haunting loneliness through re-enactment of anxious-attachment stems from the trauma of emotional abuse. As described by Bloom (1995), a striking characteristic of trauma victims involves re-enactment of the trauma. Thus, victims who have a history of emotional abuse are at risk for re-enacting this trauma of connection struggle with the hope that warm connection will be consistent. This struggle continues even to the point of dire physical danger to the victim, including fatal shootings. When threatened with abandonment, emotionally abused individuals often cling in a re-enactment of earlier trauma and in attempt to obtain warmth and connection in the face of ongoing abuse.

Social emotional abuse

Social emotional abuse occurs when there is an on-going pattern of overt and covert abuse on a social level toward a specific gender, race, ethnic or other group. Therapists at the Stone Center (Jordan *et al.*, 1991) have suggested that women are given a message in our society that connection development is not valuable, although many women spend much of their lives sharing these development skills with others. Thus, women are discounted, both overtly and covertly, by the repetitive message that their connections and nurturance are not worthy of respect, while someone involved in making a product would receive this respect.

Victim perpetrators

When individuals are emotionally abused and feel coerced into obedience to an abuser, they may engage in unlawful behavior (Loring, 1994). Traumatic bonding (Dutton and Painter, 1981) often occurs in the context of emotional and/or physical abuse. This type of bonding is demonstrated by the experience of Patty Hearst, who described the hostage-like experience and attachment with her captors (Hearst and Moscow, 1982). She struggled to obey their commands in order to receive small human kindnesses, like the opportunity to eat a meal with them or be released from a closet where she was held in captivity.

This traumatic bonding can lead to obedience in which the emotional abuse victim commits unlawful acts in response to threats of either physical harm or emotional assaults from the abuser. When a victim is threatened with abandonment, the terror of anxious attachment can result in blind obedience. Some types of unlawful behavior include bank robbery, forgery, bombings, etc. Often, the victim follows orders to complete specific tasks without an understanding of the larger violent goal. Moreover, the obedience can result in actions that are contrary to the victim's own value system.

Ritualistic emotional abuse

Emotional violence follows a script-like rendition of actions and reactions that are predictable in each situation. The repetitive use of specific mechanisms of abuse are forthcoming by each abuser in a unique style and these connect with the deepest fears of the victim. For example, many abusers threaten to abandon, either covertly or overtly, thereby attempting to gain compliance from a terrified victim with a history of emotional abandonment. Threats to harm children or pets, degradation and humiliation, criticism and put-downs may be combined to produce emotional assaults during which a victim feels annihilated. A pattern of ritualistic emotional abuse can be identified as a repetitive, torturous sequence of actions.

The continuous pattern of emotional abuse

Physical battering has been described as cyclic (Walker, 1984), while emotional abuse has been identified as continuous (Loring, 1994). The cycle of abuse in physical battering involves the build up of tension in the batterer, an explosion of violence and a honeymoon period of contrition, apologies and promises (Walker, 1984). On the other hand, continuous emotional abuse, interspersed with some warmth and kindness, is an integral part of the pattern of abuse (Loring, 1994). The mechanisms of abuse are ongoing and usually comprise a combination of overt and covert patterns of violence. The violent aspect of the continuous emotional assaults is difficult to detect, given the victim's inability to self-identify and the batterer's denial.

Chapter Two

The Identification of Emotional Abuse

EMOTIONAL abuse has been identified as a repetitive aspect of physical battering (Martin, 1976; Walker, 1984). This emotional abuse has been called nonphysical abuse (Hudson and McIntosh, 1981), emotional abuse (NiCarthy, 1986), indirect abuse (Gondolf, 1985), psychological aggression (Murphy and O'Leary, 1989), psychological abuse (Patrick-Hoffman, 1982; Walker, 1984), psychological maltreatment (Tolman, 1989) and psychological torture (Russell, 1982).

Components of emotional abuse that have been studied among women experiencing physical battering include ridicule, jealousy, threats of abuse and threats to change marriage (Follingstad *et al.*, 1990); put-downs, insults, criticism, name-calling, swearing, yelling, insensitivity (Borkowski, Murch and Walker, 1983; Ewing, 1987; Follingstad and Neckerman, 1988; Hofeller, 1982; Murphy and O'Leary, 1989; Steinmetz, 1977; Strauss, Gelles and Steinmetz, 1988; Strauss, 1974); and discounting, blaming and silent treatment (Tolman, 1989).

Emotional abuse has been described as even more painful than physical battering. Psychological degradation, fear and humiliation have been depicted as the most painful kinds of abuse (Fortune, 1991).

Ferraro (1979) described emotional abuse as detrimental to self-esteem. Additional harmful emotional abuse processes include jealousy and possessiveness (Hilberman and Munson, 1977–78; Hofeller, 1982; Rounsaville, 1978) and isolation of the woman (Douglas, 1987; Ewing, 1987; Hilberman and Munson, 1977–78; Walker, 1983, 1984). This isolation leads to feelings of loneliness on the part of the victim.

Emotional abuse can occur with physical battering, or it may operate independently in the absence of physical abuse (Loring, 1994). As an independent process, it is insidious and powerful, resulting in such symptomatology as suicidal ideation, somatic problems, depression, flashbacks, intrusive thoughts and accident-prone behavior (Loring, 1994). Yet, emotional abuse has received little attention as a separate entity. In fact, few researchers have recognized either the breaking of the spirit that occurs with this type of abuse (Fortune, 1987), or the clarity with which many battered women acknowledge that the emotional abuse is as powerful as severe physical battering (Walker, 1979). The profound loneliness that is characteristic of emotional abuse leads to utter desperation and despair (Loring, 1994).

Barriers to identification

Barriers to identification of emotional abuse are considerable for therapists, health care professionals and family/friends. Identification of emotional abuse is extremely difficult due, in part, to the lack of self-identification by the victim. When an emotional abuse victim presents for treatment, she is likely to describe a sense of despair and hopelessness along with sadness and depression, over or under-eating, excessive or poor sleeping, possible suicidal ideation, flashbacks and/or intrusive thoughts, numerous personality flaws with accompanying self-criticism and self-blame and a variety of psychosomatic problems (such as frequent bronchitis as a metaphor for losing one's voice). It is difficult for a therapist to diagnose emotional abuse in a client who is overwhelmed with self-blame. Or, when there are some complaints regarding cruel treatment, the victim still is unaware of the full extent of the pattern of external abuse.

Minor flashbacks (Loring, 1994) are common among emotional abuse victims, yet they present a challenge for therapeutic diagnosis and identification. These minor flashbacks are like petit mal seizures, an actual re-experiencing of the event with such subtle manifestations as rapid blinking, involuntary digital (finger) clutching or twitching and/or sequential shuddering (a series of shudders). Minor flashbacks often occur when an emotional abuse victim describes experiences in which humiliation and degradation contributed to the diminishment of her sense of self. Unable to identify either the abusive interaction or its impact on her, she may also lack an ability to differentiate among memories, intrusive thoughts and flashbacks.

Major flashbacks, which can be misdiagnosed as hallucinations, are similar re-experiencing of an abusive event. However, these are longer in duration and more intense than minor flashbacks. They may result in shouting and self-defensive behavior on the part of the victim, like holding her arms over her face to shield herself from criticism and verbal assaults. Following such major flashbacks, the emotional abuse victim usually 1) recalls the experience and 2) indicates that she had maintained an awareness of current reality- even while having experienced the major flashback (Loring, 1994). These are not as common as minor flashbacks.

Intrusive thoughts of traumatized, emotionally abused victims are difficult for either a therapist or the victim, herself, to recognize. Ashamed of a seemingly illogical behavior, victims often hide these repetitive thoughts from others. When discussed in therapy, intrusive thinking can be misdiagnosed as obsessive-compulsive behavior. On the contrary, intrusive thoughts are a symptom of trauma. Humiliating and degrading words and images swirl around the victim's thoughts with all of the power of trauma induced by wartime atrocities and physical battering. The traumatized victim re-experiences emotional abuse during intrusive thoughts and flashbacks while, at the same time, struggling to understand the emotional assaults and re-attach to the abuser. Reaching for an end to the trauma and experiencing a sense of emotional abandonment by this failed attempt at reattachment, the escalation of emotional abuse continues for the victim.

Thus, barriers to identification include the therapist's difficulty in recognizing major/minor flashbacks and intrusive thoughts, as well as the victim's inability to recognize that she is experiencing these symptoms. The victim's recognition often occurs when a therapist asks, "Are you simply describing that event, or do you actually feel as if it is occurring even as we are now talking?" A victim experiencing flashbacks will usually answer that the event seems to be reoccurring. She may ask for reassurance at that time in regard to whether this is "crazy."

Another type of barrier involves discounts of the victim by the abuser, friends, or even the victim's family. These discounts often involve the abuser's minimizing his abuse: "I never meant that- you must be crazy;" or, from a family member or friend, "That's not so bad;" or, "he buys you such nice furniture." When the emotional abuse is covert, the victim is quick to believe the abuser's discounts and may internally discount her own perceptions. That is, it is not always clear to the victim that she is being threatened or emotionally assaulted.

Even if the abuse is overt and the abuser threatens to kill or holds up his fists in mock readiness to punch, a victim recounting this behavior to a friend or family member may experience either discounts or criticism for not leaving. The criticism for not leaving implies that the victim is somehow exacerbating the situation or, at best, malingering. Many well-meaning interventionists overlook the destruction of the victim's sense of self so characteristic of emotional abuse. There is no self with which to detach from and leave the emotionally abusive partner (Loring, 1994). One result of these minimizing and over-expectant reactions is that the victim stops sharing information regarding the abuse or increasingly minimizes her suffering. Thus, the barriers to identification of emotional abuse are considerable.

The observation of emotional abuse is one way in which therapists and friends recognize this type of violence. It should be identified as patterned and violent, rather than accepted as humorous or benign. The ongoing cruelty becomes an infection that involves every aspect of the victim's life.

Chapter Three

Emotional Abuse: Health Care Costs

As has been suggested earlier, emotional abuse, unlike physical battering, does not leave external bruises. Rather, the wounds are internal. The internal nature of this pain often involves psychomatic problems. The physical manifestations are metaphors for internal bleeding when the pain of emotional abuse crosses the threshold of human endurance. These metaphors for bleeding need further research, although case studies reveal a wide range of somatic suffering among emotionally abused women (Loring, 1994).

Since physical battering usually involves emotional abuse as well, studies establishing physical problems among battered women are helpful in understanding the scope of this problem. The following somatic suffering has been reported among physically battered women: Bohn (1990) has described many physically battered women as experiencing hyperventilation, chest pain, gastrointestinal symptoms, pelvic pain, back pain, insomnia and fatigue. In addition, emotional abuse victims are often characterized as experiencing asthma, upper respiratory illness, bladder problems and headaches (Loring, 1994). Further, dysfunction such as frequent urination or abdominal pain, as well as aching in joints diagnosed as tendinitis or arthritis, headaches and stomach aches have all been described as part of the pattern of sadness by emotional abuse victims. These victims are able, through effective intervention, to recognize the metaphor of their trauma and pain, such as the victim's losing her voice in the relationship where her feelings don't count.

Emotional abuse victims report that, when intrusive thoughts or flashbacks are present, they experience automobile accidents that often involve missing a stop sign or running a red light. Work-related accidents are common, because concentration is difficult when cognitive functioning is imploded by internalized abusive thoughts and images. Difficulty in concentrating and academic performance has been reported among students (Loring, 1994). This over-stimulation is a form of flooding and confusion associated with the trauma of emotional abuse. Further study is needed regarding health care costs in this area of accident-related emotional abuse.

It is not possible at this time to estimate the actual health care costs associated with illness and accidents that seem to be integrally related to emotional abuse. More research is needed to identify this costly problem. Annual estimates of the cost incurred from physical battering injuries has been reported as $44,393,700.00 per year (Womankind, Inc., 1992) and the cost of emotional abuse could well be in that range, given the injuries that occur in trauma-related accidents and the cost of medical treatment for emotional abuse-related somatic problems.

Recidivism (the repetition of injuries) has been identified as a severe problem in physical battering (American Medical Association, 1992; Dunford, Huizinga and Elliot, 1990; Sherman, Schmidt, Rogan, Smith, Gartin, Cohn, Collins and Bacich, 1992). When injuries are repetitive, the medical costs mount and the human suffering is compounded. This is also the case in emotional abuse, which is not a one-time occurrence either. Illness and accidents associated with emotional abuse are ongoing, as is their cost.

The recidivism is increased by the lack of diagnosis of physical battering. Hospital room staff has been observed and interviewed regarding contact with battered women. The attitude of the staff includes compartmentalization of the injury (Warshaw, 1989). That is, the medical personnel may diagnose and treat an injury without regard to how it occurred. This results in difficulty estimating health care costs even when the wounds are directly observable. It is even more difficult to diagnose emotional abuse with its internal wounding. The lack of diagnosis of emotional abuse with related accident injuries and somatic illnesses should be studied further to develop better diagnostic training and cost estimates.

In physical battering, there are additional reasons for the difficulty in identifying family violence and establishing health cost estimates. For example, "patient unfriendly" terminology may be used in exploring an injury: A physician questioning a patient may ask about possible "trauma" versus asking "if someone hit you" (Warshaw, 1989). A patient may be able to answer "yes" to a question regarding being hit, while the concept of trauma is unfamiliar to many people. Thus, the source of their injury goes unreported. Moreover, it has been reported that medical personnel may believe that "prying" into the reasons for injuries is inappropriate to their role (Tilden, 1989). Further battering may go unnoticed for these reasons, in addition to the reluctance on the part of many battered women to disclose the source of their injuries (Tilden, 1989).

Similarly, emotional abuse victims who suffer from chronic illness and/or repeated accidents may encounter patient-unfriendly terminology. Medical care staff may ask all of the appropriate questions regarding health care issues while omitting exploration of the social context in which the repeated accidents or illness occurs. Characteristically, medical personnel may feel that "prying" into the cause of repeated illness or accidents is inappropriate role-behavior and they may compartmentalize the illness or accident without seeing the larger pattern or possible relationship to emotional abuse.

Furthermore, many of the concepts of emotional abuse, such as overt and covert abuse, discounting, negating, despair, fear of abandonment and traumatic bonding are unfamiliar to many medical personnel triaging or diagnosing an abused person. Moreover, many abuse victims cannot disclose what they, themselves, are unaware of – their emotional abuse. And emotional abuse victims, even when the threats are overt and potentially lethal, are often reluctant to disclose the source of their emotional injury and despair. They, like physically battered women, are anxiously attached to the abuser- clinging to the hope of intimacy and ongoing warm connection. Recidivism of emotional abuse-related illness and injuries is, as in physical battering, a national problem in health care costs.

Part II

Jen: Destruction and Reintegration of the Self

Chapter Four

The Meeting: A Healing Process Begins

JEN called me up to ask for help. She described her confusion.

"I don't know what's wrong with me. I feel so sad all the time. And the loneliness is terrible. For all my training to be a psychologist, what's happening here doesn't make sense. I shouldn't feel like this. I need to consult with you."

She had been referred to me by one of her colleagues. Jen and her colleague were psychologists, both struggling to figure out what could be provoking such despair in Jen- a successful mental health professional. While Jen was truly bewildered, I think her colleague had a clue as to the problem. I had become a specialist in the area of adult emotional abuse. The colleague knew this when she suggested that Jen come to see me.

Jen was thirty-five years old and she presented with multiple symptoms: Headaches, chronic depression, difficulty in concentrating and sleeping, poor appetite and low-self esteem. A thin, attractive woman with wispy, pixie-like brown hair and large brown eyes, Jen cried throughout the interview. She sat on a couch next to my chair in an upstairs office-loft where I talk with clients.

Sobbing, Jen repeatedly expressed frustration and impatience with herself. "I feel like a nothing. It's hard to remember any qualities I really like about myself. Sometimes I feel so confused. There doesn't seem to be a basis to what I feel or think. My husband Harry is a 'find.' He's a great lawyer. His skill in the courtroom is extraordinary. I visited once and saw him win an impossible case. Well, it was impossible for anyone but Harry. I should be so happy with our life together. We live in a really lovely home. My friends envy my trips to Europe. Harry is so successful."

She stopped crying and talked earnestly about Harry's successes.

"How about you?" I asked. "Where is your happiness? Who do you feel safe and connected with?"

Jen stared at me for a while, tears streaming down her face.

"No one," she replied, "no one has really been there for me, stayed warm and connected with me. I mean, not even my mother and father. My father became angry so quickly. He yelled at me a great deal while I was growing up. My mother was depressed and seemed unable to warmly connect with me ever. Harry tries, but even in bed he talks about his cases. I seem to annoy him a lot. And my best friend Cathy, who referred me to you, is dear to me. But she's very busy and out of town a lot. When Harry yells and calls me names or ignores me, I feel like I've been hit inside. I feel so cold when he's furious."

I shook my head in sorrow, "Cold and lonely, sounds sad."

Jen stared at me for a few moments, then said, "Thank you for understanding- it's like I'm not so alone."

Buffi, my blind cocker spaniel, was curled up next to her on the couch. Jen stroked Buffi's head. "It's important to feel understood," I validated her. "Tell me more about these 'annoyances' that Harry finds in you," and I made quote signs with my fingers in the air either side of "annoyances" when I said the word. She described a great many of her behaviors that Harry had pointed out as annoying while yelling at her and calling her such names as 'selfish bitch' and 'stupid.' These behaviors included taking long showers (about 20 minutes) at night and reading in bed first thing in the morning for half an hour.

Harry would explain each time that there was no reason for her to do these things, that they were silly and a waste of time. When Jen would say they made her feel good, Harry commented that she didn't feel good at all. She had two separate car accidents while contemplating discussions about her inadequacies with Harry. Jen described herself as "coming apart at the seams and unable to make decisions." She explained her sense that "there wasn't me inside my skin, just emptiness, loneliness and ugliness."

"Terrible way to feel, like you are disintegrating, coming apart." I shook my head and looked at her. I felt sad and showed it. "But your behaviors each sound great to me, like you are trying to take care of yourself, yet be considerate of Harry," I commented after she continued to describe the behaviors that Harry found annoying. She interspersed her description with comments like, "I'm so selfish; I'm so thoughtless."

"Well, Harry doesn't like these things. He says I'm selfish. Sometimes I am so frustrating to him that he yells or throws something against the wall. Sometimes he slams doors."

"Ever hit you while he was throwing an object?" I asked.

"No, but he came close once with a fork."

"How'd you feel?"

"Scared, like when my dad use to scream at me and walk around the house slamming doors. Or he'd glare at me and then leave the house for several hours. That was the worst. He'd say, "I might not come back ever," and I was so scared. Mom was depressed a lot of the time. She wasn't real involved in my life. That was scary and lonely, too."

"Old pain and trauma revisited," I shook my head with more sorrow.

"Yes," she said thoughtfully, nodding.

"I don't hear it, your being annoying these days." I commented. "Sounds like good self-caring when you said you stay an extra half hour and read in bed each morning. Are you on time for work?" She nodded 'yes.' I asked, "In what ways do you look after or care about Harry?"

She told me about numerous kind gestures that she shared with Harry.

"And for you, what does Harry do especially kindly for you?" I asked.

She was at a loss.

"Sounds like Harry finds your behaviors objectionable whenever these behaviors don't feel good to him. You seem pretty darn neat to me. Tell me about how else Harry treats you and what feelings you have during these treatments."

Jen shook her head, amazed at the turn of events. She had been trying to show me how inadequate and selfish she was. I didn't seem to be convinced. Rather, I was very impressed after hearing how she balanced her work as a psychologist in a university system and in private practice. She also served on the boards of a few human service agencies and was a big sister to a foster child. Jen was engaged in many social activities to promote Harry's law firm. And I kept commenting on her outstanding qualities: Considerate, bright, warm, kind, involved in all kinds of volunteer work.

"Yep," I said, "looks like you're pretty sure about how lousy you are, or is that Harry's voice speaking in your mind and heart?"

"I don't know," she acknowledged.

"Emotional abuse can be overt, like calling someone a 'bitch,' or it may be more subtle and covert. One covert mechanism of emotional abuse is negative labelling- calling someone's feelings 'silly.' Then there's negation where you're told that you don't even feel the way you've just stated- you and your feelings or ideas don't even exist. And the abuser's warmth slips in and out among the abusive mechanisms." Jen nodded, looking directly at me.

"What other mechanisms are involved?" she asked.

"Projection involves blaming the other person for your own inadequacies, insecurities, or frustrations. Then there is denial, where the abuser denies having done any of this. And maybe the most painful covert emotional abuse mechanism is real or threatened emotional or physical abandonment."

"Harry says he can hardly stand anymore of 'my nonsense,' and then I ask him if he's threatening divorce. He looks innocent and says, 'Of course, not.' He gives me a hug. So often there are those crumbs. Warmth peeking out at me. But he often says he's not doing what I think he's doing and I feel frightened. I'm so tired and lonely," she whispered. Jen seemed to sag physically.

"I'm sorry you feel so lonely and sad, Jen. From the past and now." We sat quietly for a few minutes. "What are your dreams? Where are your hopes and how do you feel yearning in life?" I asked.

"What do you mean?" she asked.

"Is there a craft, hobby, some skill or activity that you love, like writing, dancing, photography or something else?"

"I love to write. I keep a journal. I've always wanted to write for the newspaper, even just an article or two, but I'm not that good."

I inquired who had made that judgement. We both nodded and smiled. "Amazing gift, that Harry," I commented, "he judges you so much, must be accurate, right?" I arched my eyebrows in a mock 'very serious' look and nodded wisely.

Jen chuckled. "Well," she acknowledged, "maybe he isn't always right."

"You sure talk like a writer," I suggested, "so articulate."

"Do you really think so?" she asked. "I'm a little afraid to believe you. I think it feels so good to see these possibilities that I'm afraid you'll go away or something."

"Let's work on understanding that there are reasons for your distrust and fear of abandonment. Your mom was away a lot emotionally and your dad sure did explode at you, making trust dangerous. It's important for me to respect your concerns. We need to work out our communication so that we're sensitive to your feelings, like it's O.K. for you to call me if you get real upset in between sessions."

"Great," Jen said. "that feels safe to me. And I sure would like to write that newspaper article. You seem to think I can do it. Maybe I can."

Jen sat forward on the couch, her eyes shining with the appearance of a hesitant, yet hopeful child, leaning forward and seeking some shred of encouragement- a crumb of warmth.

Then she stared off into space for a few minutes. Jen expressed fear that Harry would not approve of a new hobby that would take up her time, that he'd probably yell at her. She said he had yelled last night about her looks. She described what he had shouted about: Harry didn't like Jen letting her hair grow longer.

I commented to Jen, "You seemed very emotional when you were describing his having yelled that you're 'skinny and ugly with longer hair.' And when you said just a minute ago that he threw a book across the room last night, you flinched and jerked back. Are you actually experiencing and reliving this experience while you're talking about it? Or are you simply describing it with feeling?"

Jen said in answer to my question, "Yes, it seems so real when I tell you about what he said. I'm terrified, like he's actually yelling at me right now. In fact, I heard his voice yelling for just a moment, saw the anger in his eyes. But I'm talking with you- how can that be? That's happened before and it scare's me that I'm going crazy or something."

I explained to Jen that, "This is a flashback. It's a minor flashback- with full awareness of the environment. You know that you're in the present surroundings, but you experience the past traumatic event as if reliving it in the present."

Relieved, Jen nodded. "I'm not crazy, then. I was beginning to wonder."

This first interview continued for an hour and a half. We were ending it when Jen looked at me and shared her hope.

"I want to keep trying to make my marriage work. I still hope to be happy with Harry. I don't want to leave him."

"Fine," I said. "But I want you to consider growing your dream- nurturing your writing. Maybe Harry can help. How about we meet together once soon and maybe once later on- you and Harry and I. Let's have him be a consultant to your growing and becoming. You don't want to leave him behind. It's fine for you to stay with Harry. It's the abusive attachment that you want to change. Let's ask him to help change the attachment. We can embrace that wonderful person who is 'you' and offer her ways to blossom and disattach from an abusive process, not from Harry, himself. What an excited look you have about you! Your eyes are shining."

Jen nodded in fast motion. "I feel more hopeful. And I was thinking about the writing. I would love to write an article for a newspaper. Do you really think that's possible?" She continued to pet the cocker spaniel sitting next to her on the couch.

"Absolutely," I assured her, "Why don't you begin considering what kind of articles you're interested in writing? Study the newspaper. Explore different sections. See if 'perspective section' is your goal or straight news. Do you know anyone who writes for or is connected with a newspaper? Ever consider taking a writing course?"

Jen remembered that, "They have continuing education courses at a few colleges. I think I saw one on writing. I'll call and find out what kind of writing. I know a reporter with a county newspaper. I helped her with a story last year."

I asked Jen, "How about you make a lunch date with her and talk about your dream? Then let's you and I, together, share it with Harry after we have several more interviews to talk about your sense of self and this abusive process."

"I'll telephone the reporter tomorrow," Jen said in an excited tone of voice, "but I don't know if Harry will come in to see you. He thinks counseling is silly."

I asked, "Would it be all right if you asked him first, letting him know it would really help you? If that doesn't work, you can call me and I'll approach him."

"That sounds like a good plan. I feel so hopeful. I haven't felt this way in a long time."

"I'm glad you feel hopeful," I encouraged her, "but be prepared that Harry may not want to come in to talk with us. Please know that I'll contact him if he takes that position. Jen, your hope is in you and is a cloak for your own dreams. That's where it'll grow."

Chapter Five

Fragmentation

Emotional crumbs

Emotional crumbs are small bits of warmth, praise, appreciation and expressed love: A pet name, a compliment on some accomplishment, statements of worth and appreciation. While most individuals experience a fair amount of these life-nurturing ingredients, emotionally abused women enjoy so little that the image of crumbs captures the scarcity and emptiness in their lives. These emotionally abused women were, as children, seekers of emotional crumbs from nurturing figures. There was a tragic void- the absence of a secure base (Bowlby, 1988), someone being consistently available to share warm responsiveness. Confused about their own sense of worth, these abused children can become emotionally abused adults who are still seeking emotional crumbs of affirmation and validation in the form of support and encouragement from their adult partner.

Paradoxically, this partner is someone who, like the original nurturer, is often more connected with his own needs and ideas than with her. Jen's feeling of profound loneliness is based on reality both in the past and the present. She is re-experiencing emotional abuse attachment now much like the struggle for connection with her parents. Jen goes to great lengths to sustain the connection with Harry and she engages in hope that a greater degree of warmth and appreciation would be present if only she performed better, was more worthy in some way. Jen dreams of this enhanced relationship, a sense of ongoing warm connection, even when she experiences a sense of *connectional hopelessness*. However, it does not develop further than crumbs of warmth and connection, interspersed with the abusive process. The dreams continue. They are continually shattered by the emotional violence of the abuser. This death and rebirth of dreams is like the poet Partnoy's image of "crucified dreams" (Partnoy, 1992, p. 31). These dreams are dashed by the violence of others and die, only to be reborn.

The disappeared

Jen, as an emotionally abused woman, is a "disappeared," just like the political prisoners depicted by Partnoy (1992). Partnoy paints a picture of her own experiences as a prisoner in Argentina. She describes the state in which a prisoner is a 'disappeared' in that "No one, except for the military authorities who kidnaped her from her home, knows her whereabouts" (Partnoy, 1992, p. 11). Disappeared can refer to being externally held hostage and lost (so that one's whereabouts are unknown), or to the state of being internally lost in the cruel grasp of another's abuse.

Partnoy's feelings and ideas were nonexistent for her captors. These captors treated prisoners with indiscriminate torture, exercising total control over their destiny of life and death. Similarly, Jen's experience of abuse included a sense that her own feelings and ideas were nonexistent. Discounting and negation are, in fact, characteristic of the emotional abuse process.

Partnoy (1992) captures the dilemma of the disappeared whose external roots and foundation (family and friends), as well as internal beliefs, are continuously emotionally assaulted:

> screams
> torture
> that great injustice,
> roots without water
> the
> disappeared. (p. 81)

Torture can be physical or emotional- overt or covert. To be discounted, negated and negatively labeled in a pattern of abuse results in a victim's conviction that her feelings and perceptions have no roots. There is no perceived internal self. Jen experienced feelings and thoughts without a basis for them, this basis having been discounted and negated. Her ideas and feelings are roots without water- the nurturance of empathy in connection. Her self is disappeared. Jen has, in effect, been banished from herself- her aspirations, dreams, ideas and perceptions. Jen lives in a state of emotional "darkness of this banishment" (Partnoy, 1992, p. 95).

For Jen, the subtle and insidious cruelty of emotional abuse diminished her sense of self, personality and self-esteem. Jen was not able to identify the covert abuse: Harry's smirks, laughs of ridicule, ignoring and interrupting her, his sighs and disgust, Harry's telling Jen to stop clinging and being 'so needy' (when he was withdrawn and emotionally inaccessible). Continuous and sometimes interwoven with warmth, the abuse process progresses as an ongoing form of emotional torture. Like a malignant tumor, the pattern of abuse eats away at the cells of thoughts and feelings- the very core of the victim's wholeness.

So that Jen disappeared- lost the joy, confidence and belief in those qualities that had become annoying to Harry. Jen tried to hide these qualities and felt guilty about them. Ironically, for Harry and other emotional abusers, the real annoyance or disgust is with themselves and this is projected onto the victim. Jen experienced the projections of Harry as if they were negatives in herself and she internalized them.

Jen's feeling of being 'nothing' involved a state of being disappeared, where she can't remember any of her own qualities that she previously liked. Emotional abuse can lead to this type of identity confusion as part of the disintegration of the self.

The disappearance of the self results from emotional assassination- to threaten and tear apart the ideas, perceptions and dreams of another as a result of the abuser's own inner rage. This assassination of another's sense of self occurs slowly over time and results in a triangular reaction of desperation/despair/sadness and profound loneliness in the victim.

Disintegration

The result of this pattern of abuse and disappearing phenomenon on the part of the victim is a disintegration of the sense of self. The victim experiences the 'coming apart at the seams' described by Jen such that parts of the personality- thoughts, ideas, perceptions, qualities, feelings- are experienced as lost or unconnected to the rest of the person. Kohut describes this "dread of the loss of his self- the fragmentation of and the estrangement from his body and mind … indescribable states of self-dissolution" (Kohut, 1986, p. 105).

During this state of disintegration, a fragmenting victim loses a sense of meaning in life. Despair, desperation and/or suicidal ideation are common. Ewing (1987) depicts this "severe impairment of one's essential selfhood" (p. 84). He suggests that, among some battered women, "victimization becomes so severe that the capacity to function as an autonomous- psychologically integrated and self-directed- individual is lost, severely impaired, or threatened with loss or severe impairment, physical existence ('life') loses much, if not most, of its meaning and value" (p. 84).

One unique feature of emotional abuse is the invisibility of the fragmentation process. There are no broken bones during the disintegration process, no external bruises or contusions. Rather, there is a brokenness of spirit (Fortune, 1987). The wounds are internal and profound. For Jen and other emotional abuse victims, the experience is that of torture.

> The slow emotional torture which produces invisible scars is as abusive as the quick, sharp physical blows (Walker, 1979, p. 72).

Emotional abuse leads to disintegration involving intense terror and trauma. This disintegration is a form of traumatic reaction in which cohesion is replaced by confusion and utter desperation. The desperation may be manifested in a number of different ways. For Jen, there was intrusion of thoughts and images regarding the trauma.

> Long after the danger is past, traumatized people relive the event as though it were continually recurring in the present. They cannot resume the normal course of their lives, for the trauma repeatedly interrupts (Herman, 1992, p. 37).

In emotional abuse, the interruption involves repetitive, intrusive thoughts regarding the abusive incident. Jen had two automobile accidents while images of the abusive interactions intruded into her thoughts. Emotional abuse victims often experience conscious flashbacks (Blank, 1985) in which one is aware of being in the present environment. These are usually brief flashbacks in which the victim re-experiences the trauma of an emotionally abusive incident.

Jen experienced what I have called minor flashbacks, which are hidden, yet insidious and powerful. The emotional abuse victim may stare into space, rapidly blink her eyes, or describe an incident in an excited fashion- all of which can be signals that these minor flashbacks are occurring. In the next chapter on intervention with cases like Jen, it will be noted that the therapist should ask whether a client is re-experiencing the incident or only describing it. When asked, most victims are able to recognize the vivid, present and "reliving" qualities of the flashback.

Jen, like some other emotional abuse victims, twice experienced longer flashbacks- still conscious- in which she relived being humiliated by Harry in front of others and cried out in terror. Jen had an awareness of being in the present surroundings, although she, like other victims, could not stop these major flashbacks. In later sessions, Jen acknowledged experiencing major flashbacks while driving. Intervention strategies will include a discussion on such safety plans as the one developed with Jen: This involved a plan for her to pull over in a safe place until the flashback was over.

The flooding of intrusive thoughts and/or flashbacks was terrifying for Jen. When she turned to Harry for comfort, he was often unavailable emotionally. Usually the abuser is unwilling to hold the victim or create a safe emotional climate in other ways that have been communicated as meaningful by the victim. Despair and loneliness become pervasive. Jen, like other victims, became engulfed with panic.

For an emotional abuse victim, the therapist is the link to recognition of an abuse pattern- the conduit for moving from desperate hopelessness and confusion to a survivor's mode of enhanced clarity, self-integration and coping skills.

Self-blame: past and present

Jen was intensely self-blaming. Here, as with other emotional abuse victims, the therapist is a significant, non-blaming connection for an individual who has grown up being blamed for another's discomfort. A primary nurturer has perceived her as a cause for his or her misery, even when that misery was actually internal- originating in the abuser. Jen's father frequently yelled at and blamed her for a wide range of events relating to his own unhappiness. And Jen's mother was emotionally withdrawn, regardless of Jen's attempts to engage her. These efforts resulted in Jen being blamed by her mother for clinging. During her adult life, Jen has re-enacted the trauma by repeating the pattern of trying to improve herself as a response to harsh and demeaning blame, both external from the abuser and subsequently internalized self-blame. Her hope was for a better ending, a more ongoing, warm connection.

Criticism and belittling remarks, ridicule and humiliations are emotional arrows that wound and diminish the victim's self. Internalized, these destructive forces enter the mind and heart of the victim (meaning her thoughts and feelings) and are transformed into mechanisms of self-blame and self-destruction, including suicidal ideation. Jen acknowledged in subsequent interviews that she had considered suicide, but would not follow through with her plan because she didn't want to "let others down."

Self-alienation and other-alienation

Disintegration, attempts to achieve connection with a rejecting and demeaning other, internalized self-blame and loss of the sense of self lead to self-alienation. Jen was alienated from her self, toward whom she feels no warm connection. Rather, there is self-blame and periodic loss of sense of self in reaction to emotional abuse. The self-blame is different from 'being disappeared' in that there is a sense of self toward whom the victim feels anger and disgust.

She is also alienated from others, like Harry, who does not see or hear the person who is Jen. Rather, he hears his own feelings and ideas, reacts to them as if they reside in Jen, and behaves as if Jen's feelings are unimportant or do not exist. Unable to understand this process, herself, Jen cannot explain it to others as a means of connecting with them when she is in the most pain. This desperate feeling of pain is characteristic of the emotional abuse process.

Chapter Six

Reintegration

Recovering from trauma

Just as establishing physical safety is the first step in helping battered women, the development of emotional safety is a primary and crucial aspect of healing for emotional abuse victims.

> Effective intervention and treatment of intrafamilial violence begins with the recognition of the primacy of traumatic events. The aim of treatment is to restore a modicum of safety and control and begin to heal damaged or shattered bonds ... The initial task is to reestablish physical and emotional safety (Krugman, 1987, p. 144).

Intervention must take into account the emotional trauma that is repeated, incident after incident. Words and actions cut through the relational bonds like knife wounds, and the brokenness of the spirit is an invisible fracture of trust and connection. Unidentified and unnamed, the abuser's unchecked danger results in a victim's terrified and desperate clinging- the sought after source of comfort, connection, and safety is, in fact, the source of harm. This is an important consideration in intervention. As Jen noted later in therapy, "My source of security was my source of harm. No wonder I was confused."

Recovering from the trauma of emotional abuse is an ongoing process, a life-long journey of a vulnerable survivor. The therapist is a coach, guide, and interpreter of pain. The emotional abuse victim begins healing through validation- recognizing the pattern of abuse- and begins to disattach from this abusive process. The tool of disattachment is the craft, educational endeavor, or dream selected by a victim. It becomes the symbol of her pulling away from the abuse and reinvesting energy into a productive, hopeful endeavor. The craft, dream, and/or endeavor is the conduit through which she will connect with others- nonabusive, encouraging, hopeful attachments. For Jen, writing the newspaper article for a small, county newspaper was exciting and hopeful, a thrilling experience of discovery about her own skills and others valuing her.

Thus, two key components of recovering from trauma involve restoring the self and disattaching from the abusive process. When Jen said that she wanted to stay in the abusive relationship, my wish for her involved a relocation of hope- a redirection of hope toward her own growth and craft. This would replace unrealistic hope of drastic and immediate change in the abuser. I invited her to feel welcome to stay in the relationship. Therapy is not aimed at dissolving love. Its goal involves identifying the abuse pattern and resulting fragmentation while embracing disattachment and reintegration skills. At some point in the future, a survivor will make decisions regarding ending or continuing with the relationship. And she will do so with a richness of self that will guide her well.

Validation

Validation by the therapist is one of the most important aspects of therapy with emotionally abused individuals: Validation of the abuse process, of the abuser's violent behaviors, of the normal reaction involving reaching out for comfort from a loved one, of the subsequent rejection and trauma on the part of the victim, and the natural tendency among trauma victims to cling for comfort (van der Kolk, 1987). All of this must be explained and clarified by the therapist through the validation process.

Validation should be the first therapeutic tool utilized with emotionally abused women. Each of their strengths, unique qualities, and accomplishments must be met with positive responses, enthusiasm, belief, and encouragement by the therapist. The role of the therapist is that of a mirror, an empathetic other who reflects the very self of the client. Empathy is crucial for a fragmenting, disintegrating self (Kohut, 1986). The therapist's empathy begins a process in which the client's 'self parts' and qualities are recognized and brought back together into a cohesive whole, who is the human client. And the growth of the client's trust in the therapist embraces her transformation from a fragmented, helpless victim to an integrated and growing survivor. This is a process of *reconstituted connectional experience*. Jen described this experience as relating to another person (her therapist) in a new way so that a blending of herself takes place, similar to "when I am cooking and all of the ingredients blend together and form a delightful dish with an identity of its own."

Humanistic therapeutic endeavor

When working with an emotionally abused client, it is valuable for the therapist to share empathy and human connectedness. The therapist should self-disclose relevant feelings and experiences that are appropriate to helping the client in order to share on a meaningful level when reaching out to a client caught in waves of despair that threaten to smother the sense of self. The humanistic connectedness offers a hope of healing for a disintegrating individual. This does not include any sexual or other inappropriate interaction with a client.

For the emotional abuse victim, healing involves feeling safe while sharing one's inner dreams, hopes, and aspirations:

> Healing occurs when we as therapists enable patients to be more fully who they naturally are. Connections are formed with more facets of their inner lives (Shainberg, 1983).

Disattachment

The second therapeutic step has begun: Jen embarked on a journey with her therapist to discover dreams and hopes. They were the vehicle through which Jen was crossing the gully of despair and desperation- pulling away from the abusive process.

Jen and her therapist share this vehicle in the therapy process. Because of the past emotional abuse and abandonment by her parents, Jen had a transference experience toward the therapist. She initially felt distrust and fear of abandonment. During therapy, this was discussed, accepted, and placed in the context of what she had been through. The therapist and Jen hope for and work together on Jen's experiencing a more secure base in their relationship.

It is valuable to spend an hour and a half in therapy sessions with emotional abuse victims. It takes them that long to attach and share their wounds, then disattach. Jen's feelings have long been denied in the form of disconfirmations (Bowlby, 1988) by her parents and Harry regarding her perceptions. She needs a great deal of validation as she slowly learns to self-validate.

The emphasis is

> on the interactions of patient and therapist in the here and now, and … the only reason for encouraging the patient at times to explore his past is for the light it throws on his current ways of feeling and dealing with life (Bowlby, 1988, p. 141).

Thus, for Jen and other emotionally abused clients, therapy involves exploring the

> working models of self and attachment figure … and restructuring … working models (Bowlby, 1988, p. 141).

In addition, the technique of *retrospective recall* involves helping the client to relax and allow a free association of memories regarding past traumatic emotional abuse. Delving into these memories in more depth, the flashbacks that are experienced form an index of past patterns of abuse experienced by the victim. These patterns are re-enacted in the present in an attempt to resolve them. During the current abuse, additional trauma produces additional flashbacks and other trauma symptomatology. These flashbacks are part of the journey- the recognition, working-through, shedding of the grip of abuse, and breaking free to disattachment as a survivor. Disattachment for Jen and other emotional abuse victims occurs not only once, but over and over again. There is a continual need to separate from abuse and reintegrate the fragmenting sense of self. Thus, there is a blend of focusing on the present and reaching back into the past as a journey toward becoming a survivor.

Jen, encouraged by my validation, was helped to develop skills in the area of her dream- writing. Actualizing this dream involved her pulling away from- disattachment from- the abusive attachment process over and over. The seeds have been planted for the blossoming of her crushed self. This is a vital aspect of healing- new activity and feedback from others with whom she will become connected during this writing process.

No where is there any suggestion that Jen should "detach" from Harry, as suggested in the codependency model (Porterfield, 1989). Not possible. She initially doesn't have an intact self with which to detach. She is not codependent. Her sense of self is, to a large extent, nonexistent. It is difficult to separate from the world of the abuser, who judges by what feels good and bad to him and does so through a language of abuse that projects blame and negative meaning onto a confused victim.

The abuser shares no (or very little) empathic connection with the victim. Rather, the abuser is focused on his own needs, perceptions, and feelings. Thus, Jen felt unwhole, yearning for connection, and willing to go to great lengths to achieve this connection. Here is a climate that is not conducive to disattachment. Believing Harry's criticism, Jen was self-blaming and attempted to improve her own behavior in order to have a richer connection. Jen could initially only criticize herself, unable to identify the emotional abuse that she was experiencing.

The victim's self must first be rediscovered and/or regrown. The actualization of dreams in the form of new activities is an active vehicle toward this end. The dream, activity, or craft is both the glue that will help draw the lost parts of the self together and the vehicle through which disattachment from the abusive process can occur. And the retrospective recall provides a means of escaping from the re-enactment of past trauma. If she chooses, the victim can stay attached to the abuser in a different way, one in which she embraces her own growing self and quickly disattaches when his emotional abuse and her disintegration begin.

The role of hope in intervention with emotional abuse

Despair and desperation result when the victim's hopes for a responsive relationship are continuously unfulfilled. She cannot embrace what is most important to her- "a secure base" (Bowlby, 1988) with her partner. The victim yearns and wishes for consistent warmth and responsiveness.

However, criticism, belittling, and demeaning are around each corner. The victim's hope is interwoven in a pattern of attempts to make consistent the intermittent crumbs of warmth and intimacy from an abuser. It is an impossible task. Her grief over continually losing the warm connection is real. Yet, giving up on such an endeavor involves grief and rage on the part of a victim whose childhood was likely to have been pained in a similar manner, lacking a sense of 'being there' by a nurturing attachment figure. To give up now is to recognize the hopelessness of changing the past. This involves sadness and realistic grief over a lost childhood filled with emotional abuse.

Yet, Jen's only realistic hope is to move from being a victim, with unrealistic hopes for the relationship, into becoming a survivor of emotional abuse with new coping and attachment skills- a survivor developing her self-system. Learning about and working through the abuse pattern and trauma (past and present) and disattaching from it- this is a hope that will allow her to leave or stay in the relationship, either way maintaining her own integration as she heals from inner wounds.

Working only with the victim

The victim, herself, can be worked with during the entire course of therapy without necessarily involving her abusive partner. I have done this on a number of occasions. Perhaps the victim did not wish to include the abuser who frightened her and inhibited spontaneous sharing. A few abusive partners have refused to participate in this type of treatment. Lastly, some emotional abuse victims may simply prefer to work alone as the lost sense of self is recovered.

Some victims of emotional abuse are not currently in a relationship, yet they may feel overwhelmed with past emotional abuse and its aftermath- a lost sense of self, recurring trauma symptoms, and a pervasive sense of sadness and loneliness. The intervention strategies that are described for victims currently in a relationship are also helpful for these individuals, including reintegration of the self and retrospective recall.

When the victim is not in a relationship, she still suffers from past emotional abuse wounds. These wounds may be inflicted by parental violence, subsequent partners, employment situations, and/or educational experiences (as with emotionally abusive teachers/professors). This model of intervention is useful in that the loss of self can be identified and explored along with growth-producing therapeutic experiences. In addition, the patterns of abuse must be understood in order to disattach not only from past abuse, but also from the internal manifestations from these painful memories. Thus, a victim who is separated from the abuser can spend a deal great of time with intrusive thoughts, memories, and even flashbacks to the abuse. Clinging to the hope of more fair and kind treatment, the victim talks about her experiences, re-experiencing the hurt, sadness, loneliness, grief, and anger. Disattaching from the abuse is an issue even when the abuser is no longer present.

And the internalized voice of emotional abusers is so loud and intrusive that a victim can be paralyzed, grief-stricken, and panicked. This is difficult for most people to understand, so these victims often are told to "detach," get on with their lives, or work through their grief. These are rarely possible processes in the midst of trauma.

Planning for disattachment

"Jen, I invite you to begin identifying the pattern of abuse- the ritualistic emotional abuse." I suggested to her during our second session (without Harry). Jen figured out that first came his sigh, then tapping of a foot, followed by a subtle criticism, and then he would withdraw emotionally. "And what is your response?" I asked her.

"I always hold on tighter. I cling to him. 'Please hold me and talk to me,' is my standard pitch. The more I ask, the more he goes away emotionally. I feel so desperate sometimes. I hate to admit it, but I've thought of killing myself."

"Jen," I answered, "I understand that desperation leaves you without hope, so it makes sense for you to consider destroying what has already been diminished- yourself. Does that make sense to you?" I asked Jen during the second session. Jen expressed her belief that this self-destruction was an outer manifestation of the destruction flowing from emotional abuse. We made a 'no suicide' contract where she would not harm herself intentionally or "by mistake." Safety measures for driving were discussed. She committed to taking a break from driving and finding a safe place when experiencing flashbacks, in order to avoid car accidents "by mistake" and induced by trauma. The therapist models and coaches, helping the victim to begin a process of self-validation that will grow out of the validation by the therapist.

Once the emotional abuse pattern has begun, Jen must tear herself away from the geographical and emotional setting.

> Jen, when you hear the sigh and foot-tapping, it is time for you to excuse yourself and run over to the other room where you have prepared a space for your writing projects. It is important to prepare Harry for this, so that he doesn't feel abandoned and angry. Let's tell him how you are going to do this when we meet together next week, O.K.? So you can begin observing the sequential pattern of abuse- the ritualistic emotional abuse- during this week and fixing up your workspace. What do you think?

Jen expressed excitement and hope. We discussed the internal focus of her hope- in her craft and self.

Engaging the abuser as a consultant

For those emotional abuse victims currently in a relationship, involving the abusive partner as a consultant can be a valuable therapeutic endeavor. Since Jen wished to remain in the relationship and Harry agreed to participate, I engaged Harry as a consultant for her craft development after having worked with Jen on validation and disattachment. Her explorations about writing symbolized her self-growth and became a tool for disattaching. She would disattach and become involve in her writing. Harry was invited to an interview by Jen. If he had refused to attend and if Jen and I had believed that his participation was essential, I would have reached out to him, letting him know that he is a very important part of this process. While not allowed to control her growth, he was included in terms of asking his advice and requesting his cooperation when she purchased a laptop computer. I monitored his consultation to ensure that the growing skills and craft-development remained under her guidance and control. This is important when violent control and destructive power are underlying dynamics in an abusive relationship.

There are times when an abuser is so resistant, that only the victim is available for therapeutic intervention. Harry initially refused to come to a therapy session, as Jen had predicted. I called and talked with him. He described himself as "too busy to be involved in girl talk." When I explained that his participation and consultation would help his wife, he agreed to talk with me.

I told Jen about the conversation, and she was delighted:

> You aren't letting him get away without participating. It's important to me that he be part of this.

Harry would become part of the recovering team for Jen and for their relationship. I suggested to Jen that she could apply sports strategies to human relationships, like encouraging Harry to connect with her in a similar way that athletes connected with team-mates, and we both laughed. More and more, Jen's whimsical sense of humor returned and was heard during our sessions. I had learned in talking with Harry by telephone that sports metaphors were both appealing and understandable to him.

During the session with only Harry and me, Harry talked about his aspirations for the future. At one point, he told me about his father, who had put him down for not being the star baseball player in high school and college. Harry was the top football and basketball player.

"Your father- impossible to please," I had commented and he had agreed. "Must have been frustrating for you," I added.

"Frustrating and depressing," he had confided. "I think I'm too critical of others, including Jen."

I told him that I really needed his help as a consultant a time or two in Jen's counseling, and he readily agreed to join us the following week. Why the switch from unwillingness to eagerness to participate in therapy? Perhaps meeting me in a nonthreatening way allowed for him to build some trust and comfort in sharing. And we spent some time talking about both his love of sports and how he could become a better team-mate in his relationship with Jen.

Later, during the joint session, I encouraged Harry to talk about Jen's strengths by asking questions like, "What do you love and admire about Jen?" I also asked Jen about which of Harry's qualities she loved. When she began to discuss her future goals in writing, Harry started to sigh and foot-tap. I said, "My word, I play the drums but your foot-tapping is getting as loud as my playing, so I can hardly hear Jen. I think that's emotionally abusive to do that, like you are saying nonverbally that what she's talking about is silly or unimportant."

He looked at me thoughtfully. "Well, it is silly," he admitted.

"Your wife is discussing becoming a writer. This is a heart-felt dream. Harry, it's abusive for you to discount it. Besides, Jen may make a bunch of money. Or maybe become well-known. She could teach people a lot by what she writes. I read some of her writing, and I think she really has talent. Have you read any of it and encouraged her? Please don't sigh and tap loudly while she's talking, or you'll hurt her feelings and discourage her. I don't think that's helpful for your relationship. And it certainly needs to be improved as good teamwork."

He stared at me, then turned to Jen. "I don't mean to hurt your feelings. I get impatient sometimes when you're talking. I don't know why."

I asked if this was a life-long pattern, and Harry acknowledged that it was- he and his father had both become impatient and criticized his mother when she talked.

I suggested, "People can learn ways of interacting, but I don't want you to criticize Jen, like indicating that her ideas are silly. I'd like you to own your feelings and say that you feel impatient."

Working with the abuser, I form a team-bond, designating him as a consultant. His abuse is labeled, and I request that it change from abusive behavior to appropriate responsiveness.

Harry needed to own his behavior and be responsively encouraging to Jen. I repeatedly told him that he was part of the team, and I needed his consultation and support. This was an attempt to model- for the survivor- the coping skills of 'inviting' (in a firm, authoritative manner) the abuser's participation and cooperation, while indicating that further abuse will not be tolerated. It will result in disattachment. Some survivors like to say this outright to the abuser.

The therapy session is an opportunity to practice setting limits, along with communicating how she would like his feelings and wishes to be expressed. He, too, is invited to make requests to her in a respectful, noncritical manner.

If things don't go well during this interview, I may turn to the woman and say, "You know, this may be as good as it gets." And then, facing the man, "I don't think you're going to change your pattern of abuse." This is unusual, because most abusers make an effort to change some of their behavior. We are open in acknowledging together that the abuser sometimes forgets and becomes emotionally abusive. I refer men who are open to further change to groups focusing on abuse, although it in uncommon for these men to follow through with additional therapy unless the woman is threatening to leave them (which also seems to be uncommon in the early stages of therapy).

I join with Jen in asking Harry to consult about her writing. I ask Harry, "Would you please support her disattaching from you, literally scooting out of the room and reattaching herself to her writing project, when you are abusive?"

Harry explains his concern that she might go away forever. Abusive individuals are often afraid of abandonment, themselves. Jen reassured Harry that she has no intention of leaving him. Then Harry agreed for Jen to disattach. I asked him what ways he might assist Jen in her quest to become an author. He suggested that he should be less rigid about her being home each night. "Maybe," affirmed Harry, "Jen could take a writing class that meets once or twice a week. Jen and I both complimented him on this idea, and he proudly beamed. Harry suggested that he could buy Jen a computer and printer, and then he began to decide what type he'd buy.

I called a halt to his taking control and compared the situation to his negotiating with another lawyer or a judge. I suggested that he call Jen, "Judge Jen," for the moment, and explained that it might help him to become less the boss and more the offerer. We laughed when he used the "Judge Jen" label and offered her a computer. Jen thanked him and accepted his gift on a condition: She would do research about computers, talk with him, and then she would select the computer and printer. I modeled negotiation for him, telling Jen about my lap-top computer that I like so much and wondering if she'd like to shop and explore lap-tops.

I warned them: This process isn't easy in that his abusive behavior and her clinging might reoccur. It is helpful to protect each of them from feelings of failure.

Harry started to put Jen down for sometimes clinging "in a ridiculous and child-like manner," and I stopped him by my having a dramatic coughing attack. My exaggerated coughing continued for a moment while I clutched the chair.

"What's the matter?" he asked, grinning at my exaggeration.

"I'm developing an allergy to your putting her down," and I gave him a dramatic sneeze to round off my allergic reaction.

"O.K.," he acknowledge laughing, "I can take a hint."

Jen was grinning.

I looked at Jen, then at Harry: "She clings when you emotionally withdraw. Your withdrawing is an abusive behavior coming from someone who loves her a lot. How about you cut out that withdrawal, Harry. Who withdrew from you, Harry, when you were growing up?"

Harry recognized that he does withdraw, and Jen sat forward in her chair with an expression of interest. She told me during our next session that the clarity and naming of the abuse left her feeling elated and relieved, hopeful about learning to identify it herself. When Harry then told us about his mother's tendency to withdraw and how "awful it felt to me," I asked him if he wants Jen to feel badly, and he said not, that he'd work on it. Harry added that he isn't aware when he withdraws and asked Jen to tell him when he does it.

I suggested that Jen could quickly alert him. Then, if he chose to do nothing about stopping the withdrawal, that Jen needs to immediately disattach so that she wasn't put in the position of attempting to draw warmth out of him. I told them that the futile, frustrating, and desperate attempt to draw warmth from and connect with a resistant other is clinging. And Harry's responsiveness and warmth is his responsibility. Jen volunteered to acknowledge with Harry when she experienced him as withdrawing and then to disattach if necessary.

Subsequently, Jen reported that Harry was trying to be less abusive and more responsive. She became quicker at identifying the developing pattern of abuse in order to disattach. Jen left the room to write when he became critical or withdrawn. She described Harry as denying his behavior less frequently when she pointed it out to him.

He purchased the computer and printer of her choice and encouraged Jen when she began a bi-weekly evening university course on writing.

Reintegration versus fragmentation

When the emotionally abused woman comes apart or fragments, she feels confused, unwhole, and traumatized. An important goal of therapy is the journey toward reintegration- a coming together of her lost and diminished parts. At the same time, some new parts are developed though the use of reintegration tools which will be discussed later in this chapter.

Anxious attachment (Bowlby, 1973, 1979, 1988)

I prepared Jen for slips- forgetting to notice the abuse pattern until it is too late, and she is clinging to him with desperation. "Natural," I assured her, "Since your whole life-long pattern has been characterized by anxious attachment described by Bowlby (1973, 1979, 1988)- a fear of abandonment and a desperate clinging to the loved other in the hopes of attaining consistent warmth and responsiveness. The absence of this secure base of warmth from nurturing figures during childhood has established the clinging, anxious pattern of reaching out to and embracing another, more and more as this other threatens to, or actually abandons."

Jen nods thoughtfully, and we discuss this theory as a knowing smile appears on her face. "That sounds like me, the clinging," she affirms.

I tell Jen that she is vulnerable to Harry's withdrawal and unresponsiveness. Rejection and emotional abandonment during childhood by her mother has set the stage for this vulnerability:

> attempts to influence his parents to give him more time, attention, and understanding have met with nothing but rebuff and punishment (Bowlby, 1979, p. 158).

Disattachment is hindered by the anxiety and terror in attachment between an emotional abuse victim and the abuser. This terror is characterized by the victim's fearful, frozen, and immobilized behavior (Symonds, 1975). Furthermore, Symonds depicts a tragic paradox in which a victim feels such overwhelming terror that she clings to the abuser- the violent person who has placed her in danger, such as the hostage-taker. This paradox is also found among both physically and emotionally abused women- holding on tightly to the source of harm. Jen and other victims need help in recognizing this in order to move toward the process of disattachment. The therapeutic clarification and subsequent understanding and enhanced disattachment skills are an integral aspect of intervention with emotional abuse victims.

In addition, disattachment is further impeded by the desperation and despair growing from the victim's disappointed hope that a solid and secure base will become available in the relationship with an abuser. Clinging to the abuser, the victim's hopes are repeatedly dashed. But, unless these unrealistic hopes can be let go, disattaching from attempts to connect will be difficult to stop. Intervention involves sharing these patterns and issues with the victim, herself.

Feeling overwhelmed and hopeless about the relationship, the victim paradoxically experiences repeated episodes of hope in which she clings to her partner. The result is a despairing sense of loss. The emotional abuse victim is at risk for suicidal ideation or other self-destructive behaviors unless the abusive process can be identified and disattached from. Disattaching is difficult until the craft or endeavor is selected, and disattachment skills are developed. Intervention must include repeated evaluation of suicidal potential, as well as warnings regarding the risk for some victims to become victim-perpetrators, obeying orders that result in criminal behavior.

Jen found it very helpful to hear explanations regarding the connection between adult emotional abuse and attachment anxiety, suicidal ideation, panic, terror, paralysis, hopelessness yet periodic hope and clinging:

> I thought I was going crazy. I really believed I was losing it. Now my clinging makes more sense to me. It's a reaction to his denigration and abandonment. I'm not so angry at myself. There's hope that I can change.

Restoring the self

I always apologize to an emotional abuse victim for the need for her to change, when she is not perpetrating abuse. To Jen, I said,

> I am really sorry to ask you to examine your behavior, identify the sequence of behaviors in the abuse pattern, and disattach. That's a lot of work. to ask of a victim. I know that we'll meet with Harry. I'll be asking him to change as well. Please know that you're doing nothing wrong. Your traumatic clinging and attempts to please him are very understandable and have been your defenses and patterns for all of your life in dealing with abusive people. I see such hope in you. That is why I ask for your growth and disattachment from abuse- to protect you and help develop more fruitful coping, survival, and creative skills. That is the reason I request your tolerance for the pain of retrospective recall, and invite your openness to a 'reconstituted connectional experience.'

Since emotionally abused women are frequently demeaned and criticized, the therapist's explanations about anxious attachment and directives regarding disattachment should be framed as a means of restoring an abused and diminished self.

Integrative self-naming and the council

I suggested to Jen that she name her self-parts or qualities: She named the fun-loving part of her self "Rollercoaster"; the caring and kind part she named "Blanket" (because someone told her that she 'blanketed' them with caring); and "Whiz" was the writer part of her. Jen made lists of these parts and added to them, creating a council in which each part gave input for decision-making and supplied comfort for her profound loneliness and sadness. Jen commented on this reintegration process:

> I feel like naming my parts helps me. I read over the paper that lists them when I feel like I'm coming apart. I can disattach from the abuse. I study my list and remember them pretty well now. I think about each of these parts when I'm trying to reintegrate. Sometimes I imagine one of them comforting me. "Soother" is my comforting part. I feel her presence when I leave the room where the abuse is happening. This is if he starts his signs and foot-taps. I make tea. I don't lose myself. It feels like I'm restoring myself before his criticism drains me out.

It is important for a therapist to rule out the possibility of a client experiencing a multiple personality disorder before engaging in this self-reintegrating technique. It could be confusing to such a client. This tool is helpful in controling both anxious attachment and clinging.

Embracing wholeness

Jen had lunch with her journalist friend who recommended that she submit an article to the county newspaper. Jen did this and it was accepted for publication. She received several calls complimenting her when the story was printed. After completing the writing course and having a few more articles published in the small newspaper, Jen began submitting and having articles accepted in magazines and larger newspapers. Her friendship circle widened and she was surrounded by validating individuals. Jen began to develop higher self-esteem and learned to validate herself.

The healer as a mentor

The therapist, as a healer, is a mentor to the emotionally abused woman, who does not know how to reintegrate her fragmented self. Furthermore, the healing process involves "reintegrating the survivor into the community" (Herman, 1992, p. 217), whether that community involves group therapy, craft development and application in the large community, and/or connecting with validating individuals. The therapist can explore these options with the survivor during her quest for healing.

Recovery from trauma

There are several ways in which emotionally abused individuals discover meaning in the transformation from being victims to becoming survivors. First, the identification of and disattachment from the abusive pattern is a freeing process that can be experienced as a very meaningful transformation. This includes disattachment from external abuse by the abuser and from internal abuse in which the victim is retraumatized by self-criticism, harshness or harm to the self, and/or intrusive thoughts and flashbacks. After talking about each abusive and traumatic incident, the survivor attempts to find a meaningful technique for expelling the intrusive thoughts regarding each abusive incident. I often suggest that the victim imagine placing the intrusive thought in a train car and running it across the track in one's mind until it exits. This is disattaching from internal abuse.

Herman (1992) described the potential meaning of trauma when some individuals discover a "survivor mission."

> These survivors ... discover that they can transform the meaning of their personal tragedy by making it the basis for social action. While there is no way to compensate for an atrocity, there is a way to transcend it, by making it a gift to others. The trauma is redeemed only when it becomes the source of a survivor mission (p. 207).

In addition, reintegrating the self and reconnecting with community through craft or new skilled activities infuses the survivor with a new sense of meaning, identity, and mission. Survivors reach out to others for meaningful exchanges. This out-reach may take the form of writing, video or film production, media appearances, pursuing a career or volunteer work in helping others who are abused, and other types of mission-like activity.

Jen decided to work with some emotional abuse victims in her private psychology practice. She also began to deliver community seminars about emotional abuse. Jen completed therapy with me in ten months with the understanding that she was welcome to return for consultation. Every several months or whenever a crisis occurs, Jen makes an appointment to talk with me for one to three or four sessions. Traumas are explored and worked out. New coping skills are developed. Past trauma is examined and worked through in retrospective recall. The reconstituted connectional experience with me is renewed.

It is crucial in therapy to examine the meaning that a trauma holds for an individual. Embracing that meaning and integrating it into a sense of self is a transformational challenge.

Part III

Janet: Legal Consequences of the Abuse Process

Chapter Seven

Notes From a Diary

April 8, 1993

10.00am

What will it feel like when I hold the gun tightly by its handle, aim it at my head? Press the gun against my temple. Pull the trigger. Will I know what happened? Why do I hesitate? The decision has been made. There is no hope. None. I am nothing. Less than nothing. I couldn't hate myself so much if I were nothing. I'm probably so inept that I won't even be able to shoot myself. Disgusting. I am disgusting.

I wish to be dead. For the pain to stop. It's like I'm in the dentist's office- the drill is boring into my essence, my self, whatever it is when people talk about a heart. My heart is broken. No. Shattered. I'm too tired to piece it together- a jigsaw puzzle, crooked pieces bizarrely jagged beyond belief. Exhausted. Attaching is too hard. Even having a conversation- can hardly write in this diary- my sustenance and connection. Connection to what? Some hidden piece of me that hasn't been destroyed?

They'll all know tomorrow. Michael having persuaded the entire world that we are Atlanta's perfect couple. Jet-setting around the world a couple times a year. His and hers cars- his a Mercedes and hers a Corvette. Gorgeous home in Midtown. God, I should have asked, "Where's the money coming from?" Never crossed my mind again. Once I wondered out loud. A lot of trips even for a successful lawyer. When I asked where the money came from, he wouldn't touch me or talk to me for a week. Loneliness. That's when I first thought about killing myself. Not to exist in body, as well as emotionally.

Successful lawyer in corporate plush. Best law firm, most prestigious everything for Michael. Finest Mont Blanc pen and monogrammed sleeves. Guess it wasn't enough. Said he'd been happier if I hadn't been so stupid, silly and "downright boring." Makes sense.

But those packages. I probably should have known. Visiting that man in Paris, the one with the incredible entire floor of that ritzy apartment building. Bearded and suave. Asked me to dance at the fancy restaurant we went to that night. And the woman we had dinner with in New York City- her apartment was huge and overlooked Central Park. She was elegance. Business friends, Michael had said. "Try not to look quite so frumpy and don't be so boring."

Before I had delivered the packages to each of them the second time, Michael had been so kind and warm to me. Admired my personality. Made love gently. Later, after the delivery of packages, he'd looked at me, shook his head and called me names. "Slut," "worthless," "sexless."

I'd get an ache in my throat. Like a small animal at the edge of a cliff. Waiting to cry out. Some sound of anguish. And I'd start to perspire. My stomach would ache.

The names Michael called me. Not a punch or slap- not physically. A heart-slap. They ground and cut the self of me to pieces:

> Are you wearing that outfit? Can't you do something to look better?
>
> Can you think of anything interesting to say at the party tonight?
>
> Maybe there will be some attractive women there.
>
> I feel like sex. Do it.

My car accidents while thinking about the emotional put-downs-me-squashes. Can't stop thinking. They pop into my mind. Like it's happening over again. Same terror in me. Wasn't once enough? My attempts at rejoinders. Why do I even try? Maybe to keep some small piece of my self alive, believe in me just a little. Putting my car in the wrong gear while getting off the expressway. God, going from forward to reverse in high speed. Terrifying. Lucky I didn't hit a car. All the names he'd called me swirling around in my head. Trying to make sense of it. Never could. The names like arrows aimed at my heart-coming at me right then. "Stupid," "bitch," "going to leave you." I could hear him while I was driving. "Bitch, can't you do this right one time?"

If I had been one of my clients, intrusive thinking or maybe flashbacks would have been my diagnosis. A good counselor, so they say I am. Seems even worse. A counselor trying to kill herself. Like a minister molesting kids. Doesn't fit.

The car accident. Maybe it was intrusive thoughts. I couldn't keep from trying to figure out why Michael said that: "Maybe there will be some attractive women at the party." He used to say I was attractive, when we were dating. Years ago. Lives ago. Me wearing his favorite lipstick, very expensive dress, shoes, hairdo. Why do I try so hard? He still calls me bad names no matter what I do. Always the names. The smile with his dimple. A bit of warmth dances in and out of my life. I grasp at the warmth. Hope for more.

Hope for more. No hope with a gun in my hand. Which is it?

Only a dissertation to go. Can't seem to do it. Only a year to go, then too late for the five year limit on finishing my dissertation for the doctorate degree. "Don't expect you can finish it." Michael had named the failure. Before it happened. So of course it will.

All those packages. Credit cards. Michael smuggling credit cards into and out of the country. So they say. And he'd had me carry some of the packages. Deliver some. Mail others. Pictures of me at post offices around the world mailing packages. The FBI agent showed me the pictures right after our arrest. Me clutching brown wrapped packages. Looking lost, wide-eyed, dazed.

"Business packages," he had said. "Mail them while I'm at the meeting. Think you can do that right?" The unsaid names: "Stupid, incompetent, worthless."

"You mailing credit cards?" the FBI man had said while showing me those pictures. I'd dully stared at him. Stunned. Booked. Jailed.

Out on bond. It'll all be in the newspaper tomorrow. Imagine their faces at school. It would be funny if it weren't so awful.

"People don't mail packages without knowing what's in them," the FBI agent was right. People know what they're mailing. And I'd mailed them time after time.

But it really didn't matter. Didn't matter that my best friend bailed me out and left Michael in jail. "He got you in this trouble. Let him get himself out," she had said. I spent the night with her. Now, here at home, the answer seems clear. Yet I stall. It should be so easy. The phone rings. I don't answer. Both dogs shut up in the back bedroom.

It seems my end is not taking place. Can't seem to do it. I don't know whether to hate myself. Or be grateful. Even this seems unbelievable. I feel stunned. The gun. The suicide attempt. The failure. What will it be like in jail? Yesterday in jail, a woman made a pass at me. I didn't care. I said 'no,' thanked her and shook her hand. She looked startled, then smiled, shrugged and walked away. I felt claustrophobic. Being locked up and walking through corridors with so many gates clicking shut behind me. Guess you get used to it. Guess you get used to just about anything. Even Michael's names- brillo pads caressing my insides, pulling off parts of myself with each stroke.

5:00pm

Michael in jail. His bond set at $1,000,000.00. A credit card carrier killed in Nigeria. So, the high bond. Murder and international intrigue. Thought I'd just read about such things. Imagine being part of it. Confusion, like everything's going in fast motion. Can't eat or sleep. And the thoughts, like I hear the voices or see these people and packages all over again. Or I hear Michael threatening to kill mother or my dog Snappy. Me, at home, alone, after Mother and Father's visit. Relieved. God help me. I am free. Mother came down to the police station to help Lori get me out on bond. Mother stood next to Father by the bench in the police station, not sitting down next to the man in a green suit. She is sure you can catch AIDS by the moisture in the saliva of HIV positive people. Can't let them breathe on you. She has warned me about this. Discouraging my volunteer work at the battered women's shelter.

"Might be a needle co-user among those women." She has told me over and over. Always she tells me things. Never asks what I think or feel. Her feeling is a blanket. Covers me, too. Her interior designer has AIDS. He asked me not to tell her. I agreed. They paid my bond. Took me home and assured me that it's all some awful mistake. Lori winced when Mother named the "mistake." Lori doesn't think there has been a mistake. She has to dash.

Michael. Mother and Father's hero and wonderboy. He is everyone's wonder. Boyish face and shaggy blond hair. Rugged and athletic. He is a sun in whose shadow I bask. "He's the exciting part of your life." Mother would tell me this when I expressed sadness about his emotional distance. "Besides, nobody's perfect." Mother knows these things, "You always expect too much. Mustn't be greedy." I thought about that a lot, my being a perfectionist and greedy.

My mother stayed at the house after I had been bailed out of jail. She talked at me. My father shook his head and stared out the window. Then they left. I was more lonely when they were there.

Last week, I was telling Michael that I loved him. But didn't want to do some of the kinky sex. He locked himself in the bathroom with a six-pack and the portable TV. Me pounding on the door. He wouldn't answer. I begged him to talk. Wanted him to say he loved me. Silence. I was desperate. A doctoral candidate and counselor. Pounding and weeping. Confused and clinging, How can a closed door be so upsetting? I was gasping for breath and frightened. He finally came out and grabbed me.

Michael choked me. Threatened to kill me. I was terrified, couldn't breathe. Fainted. Woke up surprised I wasn't dead. He's done it three times. Each time, I get ready to die. The first time, I said I'd prefer not to mail a package. The second time was the bathroom lock-up. Me pounding on the door. Then I forgot to mail a package one morning in Paris. I came home from shopping. He locked me in the bathroom. Then wouldn't speak to me. Later, on the way to a party, he drove the car so fast and scary. Said he'd kill my dog. Then eat him for supper. Once he smacked the little dog so hard. I got a terrible headache, hid the dog from him. Michael said next time it'd be worse. He'd kill me. Then my mother. Then my dog. The threats were so scary.

I sit alone out back on the porch swing. It's evening. The air cools.

Chapter Eight

Victim Perpetrator: Participation by the Emotional Abuse Victim

Victim perpetrator

Janet is a perpetrator. She has mailed packages of stolen credit cards all over the world.

It's not a normal criminal case. She is emotionally and physically abused. The criminal behavior is not an activity that Janet would have planned on her own. She is a counselor who returned to college to complete her doctorate. Janet has no history of criminal behavior. Rather, she has devoted years to community service and church work, as well as several years as a counselor in the school system.

While the prevalence and incidence of victim-perpetrators is unknown, any emotionally and/or physically abused woman is vulnerable to this phenomenon. That is, any abused individual can, under certain conditions, discover that she is experiencing a state of duress in which she feels compelled to obey the orders of an abuser. Coerced deviance involves the forced participation of a victim in criminal behavior. Threats to the victim, her children, pets, family members- all of these are terrifying to a victim coerced into obedience to the abuser.

Janet' lawyer called me to request a psychosocial evaluation. The lawyer asked whether she was coerced or under duress during the stolen credit card deliveries. He explained that the presence or absence of these two factors is important:

> It's really crucial in the federal system to establish whether the factors of duress or coercion were operating. Did they influence Janet's behavior so that you can address the question as to whether her actions could be considered reasonable under the circumstances?

These factors are spelled out in the federal guidelines as conditions for downward departure- a decrease in the severity of punishment. This punishment can consist of incarceration (in prison), a half-way house, home confinement and/or probation.

The roles and skills, vision and humanistic approach of the evaluator/therapist- in the therapeutic encounter and during the legal process- are crucial in understanding and helping a victim-perpetrator. And the scope of the victim-perpetrator's dilemma is symbolic of the larger social issues impacting on emotionally abused trauma victims. They have a double burden of both experiencing and explaining the trauma-driven behavior and the abuse-related terror underlying their behavior.

After spending about twenty hours evaluating Janet, I met with the lawyer and shared my clinical impressions:

> She was emotionally abused, as well as physically battered. Her life was threatened and she was in danger. Janet had been severely choked a few times and the lives of both her mother and dog had been threatened. He'd discussed killing her if she didn't deliver the packages. One time she was choked for objecting to delivering- once for not delivering. I think she was under duress and coerced. Her behavior seems reasonable to me under these circumstances.

A victim often obeys the orders of the abuser whom she loves. Bright and accomplished victims either do not question the order or do so only once. When abuse follows the question, it is rarely repeated.

And these victims see only the mini-task, like delivering a package. They do not grasp the scope and context of the ultimate and larger acts, as demonstrated by another victim-perpetrator who bought each item that she was told to purchase. When the bomb went off and killed someone, she saw the account on television. The horrible possibility occurred to her. Could she have bought the parts that the reporter kept talking about in relation to what he called the "homemade bomb?"

She asked her husband. His response was indignant.

> "Of course not, Stupid. I never made that bomb."

Relieved, she believed him. He was later charged with the crime. She was also arrested.

This difference between willful law-breaking and victim-perpetrator obedience can be recognized, especially when a sensitive lawyer hears the client's abuse and calls in a mental health professional for an evaluation. Janet's grief involved the loss of her sense of dignity and worth. This was not behavior that she would have chosen on her own. It conflicted with her values. Rather, the behavior in which she had participated occurred in the midst of her trauma.

What a paradox! A woman loves a man who leads her into incredible trouble, sometimes even pointing an accusing finger at her for the legal authorities, abandoning her after the illegal activity and/or expecting her to continue their relationship after the crime- as if no abuse had occurred. And many of the women continue to love the abuser. Some remain loyal to him. Others experience a sense of freedom when their relationship ordeal is over. They report a rediscovery of their lost self and a sense of freedom from abuse. Jail feels like a sanctuary. At the heart of this paradox is the attachment of the victim to the abuser. Janet was relieved to be free from Michael, although she felt lost without either Michael or her sense of self, destroyed during the on-going emotional abuse.

Janet could not be called a survivor at this point, because she is truly a victim- clinging to the abuser with desperate intensity that is difficult to understand and convey. Like Patty Hearst, she is a victim who has become part of the illegal process.

The Stockholm Syndrome

In the Stockholm Syndrome, a terrorist intersperses terror with kindness, creating a power imbalance for the victim (Graham *et al.*, 1988). It may be a hostage situation in which a terrorist offers food intermittently to the victim, who becomes fond of the captor, only to subsequently face threats of death as the alternative to obedience. The victim identifies with the captor and may actively enter into the captor's plot against society in order to survive (Hearst and Moscow, 1982). In a sense, Janet was a hostage struggling for nurtance and support, obeying the abuser.

Walker (1984) describes an intermittent reward system in the cycle of abuse. Tension builds up in the physical batterer. He explodes with rage, followed by a honeymoon period of gift-giving, promises and contrition. The victim experiences terror.

Traumatic bonding is a consequence of the victim's terror.

> Traumatic bonding results from the utter dependency of a terrorized person on an assailant and the resulting pathological identification wherein the victim feels benignly toward the perpetrator (van der Kolk, 1987, p. 137).

The victim's feeling is that survival is dependent on pleasing, conforming to and obeying the captor. Thus, the hostage follows orders blindly. Therapists must see beneath the obedient actions of a victim-perpetrator, like Janet, to fully appreciate the sense of her being 'in captivity' with the accompanying torture, terror and trauma.

A large part of the torture involves emotional abuse that is continuous, rather than cyclic (Loring, 1994). While the abuse is continuous, warmth and reinforcement is intermittent, similar to hostage situations and physical battering. Like a tapestry, this warmth is interwoven with discounts, humiliation, name-calling, subtle put-downs, jealousy and other forms of control. The abuse may be covert, overt, or a mixture of these two levels of emotional abuse. Much like a physically battered woman and a hostage, the emotional abuse victim grasps and clings to crumbs of warmth and comfort, yearning for connection and hoping for survival.

The adhesive nature of traumatic bonding

Dutton and Painter (1981) examine bonding in which the victim is traumatized by the behavior of the batterer, who switches back and forth between violence and the honeymoon period (Walker, 1979, 1984). This switching involves the giving and then taking away such reinforcement as warmth and praise, so that there is a pattern of intermittent reinforcement, This occurs in emotional, as well as physical abuse. The resulting traumatic bonding is very difficult to break. Desperate and lonely, Janet clung to Michael's occasional warmth.

Why didn't she see that he was using her? In fact, Janet is bright, with numerous awards for her work. Traumatic bonding cuts across ethnic, professional, religious and intelligence boundaries. It holds the unaware victim in an inescapable, suffocating grasp. This attachment grasp is universal in the emotional abuse process. The experience is that of being in captivity.

Many victims of battering and abuse struggle with low self-esteem from childhood mistreatment. Some feel uncertain whether they deserve a better kind of bonding and attachment- one that embraces their needs, feelings and ideas. And when there is diminishment, loss and/or destruction of the self, the abuse is often unseen and unidentified. Emotional abuse is usually minimized by the victim and is experienced as overwhelming desperation without a name, increasing the difficulty of breaking the bond. Unable to break this bond, Janet experienced destruction of her self along with desperate clinging.

Helplessness

Seligman (1975) described learned helplessness in which there is a sense that events are not controllable. Animals who were repeatedly shocked, regardless of their behavior, were subsequently unable to escape from the situation- even when the means for their escape were apparent. Similarly, with humans, learned helplessness has been described as occurring when there is an inability to predict the success or effectiveness of ones' actions (Seligman, 1975).

The helplessness in traumatic bonding has been described in two ways. Walker (1984) called it 'learned helplessness' and likened it to an utter hopelessness and disbelief regarding one's ability to initiate or effect any substantial life changes.

Herman (1992), on the other hand, cautions again defining a characteristic as being located internally in the victim when that may not be the case. From Herman's perspective, family violence and the resulting trauma for the victim results in nothing less than feelings of helplessness. That is, the continual futility of standing up for oneself and the physical harm that can result from such efforts cause a hypervigilance and a sense of helplessness regarding taking such initiative.

While Herman (1992) is focusing primarily on disasters, human infliction of torture, and physical battering in the family, the same dynamic applies to emotional abuse. When traumatic bonding is generated by the continuous emotional abuse interspersed with intermittent warmth and reinforcement, the victim experiences a sense of helplessness and futility. Janet's helplessness overwhelmed her at the point during which she considered suicide. She felt both hopeless and helpless, seeing no escape from the situation. And she described ongoing feelings of helplessness in reaction to Michael's abuse for several years: They had been married for seven (7) years.

Furthermore, Van der Kolk (1987) attributes helplessness- the feeling that one's actions do not relate to the outcome of one's life- to the trauma of having no safe place inside or outside oneself. In fact, there is no safety in the emotionally abusive relationship, with its mine fields of insidious, wounding denigration. The lack of emotional safety is augmented by a victim's fear of abandonment and her desperate clinging to an unresponsive or increasingly emotionally abusive partner. This was true for Janet whose desperation was highest when clinging to Michael while he behaved in a manner that was both rejecting and humiliating. She also felt a sense of having lost the essence of herself.

With the loss of the sense of self and intense self-blame, emotional abuse victims do not experience internal safety. Not only is there a lack of safety within the external abusive relationship, but internal self-criticism and self-blame create a traumatic bonding connection with oneself. For Janet, the ultimate disconnection was through suicidal ideas.

Emotional abuse within a family, couple, parent-child relationship, work situation, university or school setting, yields a sense of helplessness and diminishment of the victim's sense of self. Janet felt so lost and diminished that she wished to match this sense of nothingness with a physical act of suicide- the ultimate state of self-destruction. Michael had, in fact, been murdering her self- bit by bit. Her intended act of self-death would have symbolically completed his rageful message of destruction and control which had become internalized, although there is a piece of herself that was a survivor, wanting to be and grow. Janet survived this time. She did not pull the trigger.

If the psychosocial evaluation can validate for Janet the dilemma of self-loss and disintegration, as well as giving up hope for reintegration, then the suicidal ideation will dissipate. The therapist can provide a secure base (Bowlby, 1988):

> ... a trusted companion to provide support, encouragement, sympathy and, on occasion, guidance (p. 138).

The therapist's dilemma

There is a terrible dilemma for the therapist who works toward the completion of a psychosocial court evaluation. The client must be able to present to the court an honest view of who she was at the time of the incident(s). It is unacceptable for the therapist/evaluator to empower or assist the client in becoming outraged, angry and/or indignant at past emotional assaults. Rather, the anguish and desperation, trauma and horror, that was felt at the time of the incident(s) and at the outset of the evaluation must be honestly experienced and related when the victim-perpetrator presents herself for understanding and judgement in the courtroom.

What are the ethics of comforting, yet leaving a client in pain? Therein lies the dilemma. This must be ethical in that it leaves the client within the honesty of terrifying trauma that they have experienced and continue to re-experience: And maintaining this original trauma while awaiting trail is in the long-term best interests of the victim. To encourage healing that promotes anger and self-empowerment, working through trauma and reintegration, is to participate in removing the victim from the honest, heartfelt terror that must be witnessed and understood during the judicial process. Further healing must occur within therapy at another stage and time. The victim's wait for the second stage can be for a few months, a year, or even more. This leaves the therapist/evaluator feeling torn and distressed at the pain of the victim/client and the need for healing to occur.

Janet cried in grief and horror when she talked with her evaluator about the individuals harmed by the credit card thefts. And the death of someone participating in the criminal network filled her with dread- what if it had been her!

> I feel panicked alot. And so scared. I could have been killed. He didn't care. How could he have exposed me to such danger? Never have I felt so alone and abandoned. I know what despair really is now. Where is there any meaning in life?

It is very difficult for a therapist/evaluator not to begin the therapeutic process, a journey toward healing. Or at least to address some of the trauma issues like Janet's loss of meaning and painful despair.

We therapists are used to helping clients to experience pain and then work through and let go of it, in order to rebuild their lives. Herman (1992) accurately describes the hoped-for therapeutic transformation of the traumatic memory, "so that it can be integrated into the survivor's life story" (p. 175). This involves a process in which survivors will

> 'let go of those aspects of themselves that were formed by the traumatic environment, they also become more forgiving of themselves ... The more actively survivors are able to engage in rebuilding their lives, the more generous and accepting they can be toward the memory of the traumatized self (p. 203–204).

While this is the long-term goal for emotionally abused women who have become traumatized, the growth from a state of painful trauma to integrating the traumatic memory and letting go of the traumatized parts of the self is not an appropriate journey for a legally troubled victim-perpetrator. Rather, it is a dangerous journey that can result in her presenting an image of herself (within the court setting) that is different from the actual self-to-other interaction at the heart of the incident(s). The punishment of the victim-perpetrator is directly related to the honest, sincere, in-the-here-and-now manner with which she presents her own dilemma and trauma to those who will decide her long-term fate.

On the witness stand, Janet told the truth. As in many federal cases, there were several defendents being tried simultaneously, sitting with their lawyers next to each other. Janet responded to questions about her role in the thefts and delivery of packages.

> I know it's hard to understand. I should have known better. It was like I was in a trance, so depressed and fighting to keep every crumb of warmth I could get from Michael. All of his criticisms and robbing me of myself piled up and I drowned under the weight of it all, like there was nothing left of me. This does not excuse my behavior, not at all. There is no excuse. And I feel so badly about the man who was killed. I met him and his little boy once. I think about the little boy a lot. I can't seem to think about anything but those packages, all the time and how Michael was so mad at me if I didn't deliver them. I was stupid not to just open one up and see what was inside. How could I have been reduced to a puppet?

This is the therapist's dilemma- not to heal. Like a minister or a chaplain, to be with and support a person without necessarily helping at that time to change their perceptions or insights, their comfort level or pain. Thus, I perceive my initial role as evaluator and supporter. The support involves assistance with self-comforting and self-soothing in the midst of traumatic pain. In addition, support includes a search for meaning, a validation of the victim's pain and suffering and frequent contact prior to the court appearance (which can be prolonged and postponed for a wide array of reasons beyond the victim's control). Yet, I honestly share with her that this is not the time for growth and absence of pain. Rather, the goal is to seek comforts, supports and hope for future rebuilding of her self and life. And this is the time for honest connection with one's own anguish and despair in order to share this heartfelt trauma with those who will decide one's role and fate regarding the crime.

What to do about the flashbacks- to allow a person to experience them and know that the evaluator is present for support. Jen expressed appreciation for my presence during flashbacks, my helping her to clarify whether they were memories or flashbacks, and the sound of my voice while she was having them.

> When I see those packages and myself delivering them, it feels as if I'm doing it all over again. And sometimes I hear the voice of the man who was killed. I only met him once. Like right now, I can see his face and I feel so sad. He held my hand for a minute and told me to 'take care and stay close to home.' I never understood what he meant, but he felt so caring. I can see the warmth in his eyes.

Jen stared off into space and I commented that "I am here." I said this twice. Then Jen began to sob and I asked if this had been a memory. She said that there was a strong sense of being there in the experience, like it was happening all over again, although she could hear my voice and it was comforting. During this flashback, Jen had reached out to grasp the man's hand again, then pulled her hand back self-consciously. I normalized the situation by saying that this was a normal response to all that she had been through and I avoided using trauma terminology so that she would tell her own story in court. Diagnosing someone does not involve telling them either the diagnosis or terminology, because their testimony should not be tainted by the evaluator's perceptions. Jen's relief at the reassurance that she wasn't crazy helped without taking away her feelings, themselves.

> I appreciate your telling me I'm not crazy. I had begun to believe that I was.

Emotional abuse as an antecedent to illegal behavior

Having experienced the threat of psychological murder (Ewing, 1987) and the actual loss of one's sense of self (Loring, 1994), it is characteristic for emotional abuse victims to report desperation, obedience, emotional emptiness, despair and anguish. Janet once asked about the content of the packages and, when she was threatened with abandonment and death, she did not ask again. Obedience prevailed and she mailed the packages.

I have evaluated victim-perpetrators who were accused of participating in such crimes as bank robberies, drug trafficking, theft, social security and employment fraud and bomb murders. The dynamics are similar: Emotional abuse and possibly physical battering (but not necessarily) lead to terror, desperation and a sense of helpless obedience. While these women have acknowledged participation in the illegal activity, the impact of abuse has created a climate in which some of the victim-perpetrators have perceived no other options. There is a growing awareness and acceptance of the relationship between abuse and actions in some of the federal courts. This awareness is also evident among lawyers and judges operating in some of the state courts.

As the legal community experiences a growing recognition of this phenomenon, more and more therapists will encounter situations in which they are asked and/or required to give expert witness testimony. Thus, it is crucial for therapists to recognize the role that emotional abuse and possibly physical battering, play in the behavior of a victim-perpetrator. Therapists must also be able to evaluate and testify about it in an effective manner.

A woman may become involved in illegal behavior, like Janet's participation in credit card theft for which she faced conspiracy charges. Or the emotional abuse can lead to illegal behavior that is less obviously impacted by the abuse, such as car accidents caused by the victim's experience of flooding intrusive thoughts or flashbacks and subsequent illegal driving behavior (like driving through a stop sign or red light).

Flashbacks and intrusive thoughts

An emotionally abused woman can, like Janet, re-experience and relive the abusive episode. It is valuable for a therapist to ask whether the victim only thinks about the story that has just been related or if she feels like it is actually happening right now, again, in the present. If the victim acknowledges flashbacks at the time of the incident and currently, the therapist should normalize it, suggesting that trauma can produce these flashbacks. Thus, the victim's fear of being abnormal or crazy is replaced with a framework which helps to understand and cope with her own out-of-control behavior.

These flashbacks have been called conscious flashbacks (Blank, 1985) in that the individual does not lose touch with present reality.

However, the flashbacks have not been widely viewed as a possible consequence of emotional abuse and physical battering. In fact, emotional abuse has not been seen as leading to traumatic reactions. It can make a big difference to the fate of a victim-perpetrator when these traumatic reactions are documented, along with the patterns of emotional and possibly physical abuse impacting on the alleged criminal activity.

The hope, for Janet, involved presenting this psychosocial documentation of flashbacks, intrusive thoughts and other traumatic symptoms along with medical reports regarding treatment for battering- to probation officers, the prosecuting attorney, the jury and the judge. The defense attorney established a strategy in the hope of obtaining either acquittal or probation for Janet. He asked me to write a psychosocial evaluation report to be utilized in the attempt at downward departure of her punishment.

It is important to provide support for emotionally and/or physically abused women awaiting trial. For these victims, there is a crucial need to honestly express to the judge and jury the total range of trauma symptoms in their own voice. Thus, the evaluator should not normalize trauma symptoms (as discussed previously), use such terms as 'trauma', 'flashback', 'syndrome', or alter the honest presentation of trauma among these victims awaiting trial. Documenting interviews with family, friends, employers, ect., as well as reviewing police, FBI, and other reports (including any medical or therapeutic documentation of trauma and abuse) is important for the evaluator.

Chapter Nine

The Therapist as an Expert Witness in Federal Court

Establishing the symptom cluster and diagnosis

Intrusive thoughts are often misdiagnosed as either an obsessive feature or a "stuckness" in the grief process- holding onto some person or other loss, rather than grieving and letting go of the lost object. Intrusive means just that: The thoughts intrude into thinking such that it is beyond the victim's control.

I always leave at least 2 hours for the first interview with suspected emotional abuse cases and at least 1 and 1/2 hours per subsequent session. These victims have to weave their way through a maze of intrusive thoughts and flashbacks, which are often presented in exquisite detail and with profound pain.

The therapist must consider the legal system when translating therapeutic skills to the courtroom. The terms I use in forensic work are "psychosocial evaluation" and "ongoing support." In some states, it is against licensing laws to use the term "psychological" if one is not a licensed psychologist. The same caution would apply for psychiatrists and psychologists when using certain terms, now that many states are moving toward licensing by function (practice laws). That is, only certain professions are allowed to claim specific skills and functions, these being spelled out by licensing boards. The larger issue involves definition of the therapist's role in a forensic setting where clinical skills are not sufficient to be effective in evaluating and helping a client.

Another caution for mental health professionals who testify in court cases involves the value of these professionals making time for their own consultation with a lawyer who specializes in the area of professional performance and licensure. Going over business cards and standard techniques of therapy, testimony, etc. is valuable to identify any potential legal problems.

The therapist may be asked to evaluate a new client or- whether she wishes to or not- may receive a subpoena requiring court testimony in regard to an ongoing client. This therapist must have a criteria or a foundation for the evaluation. Many psychologists use tests, while counselors, clinical social workers, and psychiatrists often utilize an interview evaluation based on the Diagnostic Manual of the American Psychiatric Association (DSM-IV) (American Psychiatric Association, 1994).

I use this Diagnostic Manual, exploring with the client to ascertain whether the Post-Traumatic Stress Disorder has been present in the form of such symptoms as flashbacks, intrusive thoughts, confusion, hypervigilance, sleep disturbance, depression, feelings of helplessness and hopelessness, and amnesia- in which parts of the abusive experience and incident are not remembered (American Psychiatric Association, 1994).

DSM-IV recognizes the chronic aspect of ongoing abuse. In addition, Herman (1992) discusses the chronicity of some types of trauma, such as family violence.

The Battered Woman Syndrome theory and concepts (Walker, 1979, 1983, 1984) are also valuable in establishing a basis for understanding why an abused woman stays in the relationship and experiences helplessness. Important concepts in this theoretical framework include low self-esteem, a history of abuse, the cycle of violence (the abuser's build-up of tension, explosion, and honeymoon period) that keeps a woman hoping that the honeymoon phase promises will become reality, and the deep conviction that she cannot change the situation (learned helplessness). There may also be fear of harm or death (as threatened by the batterer) if she leaves.

Thus, the therapist engaged in developing a forensic evaluation establishes the foundation, terminology, and conceptual framework with which to put forth a diagnosis, including the cluster of symptoms and the impact of these symptoms on the victim's behavior. The therapist's testimony must include accurate facts, like the dates and total hours of the therapist's evaluation, when the incident (alleged illegal activity) occurred, all of the information surrounding the incident-related events and involved individuals, as well as a psychosocial history that would help to explain the woman's behavior. It is helpful for the expert to review hospital records and other documentation of abuse (like interviewing family members, friends, neighbors and employers). Objective findings related to the possible existence of coercion, duress, and diminished capacity are all relevant.

The expert witness presents a scientific body of information not readily available to the average citizen. The professional manner in which this information is presented can be important in establishing the credibility of the expert and painting a vivid, human, accurate picture of a victim-perpetrator.

Style of testifying

While each individual has a unique style of testifying, it is important to be credible and to avoid becoming defensive. When attacked in an effort to minimize my professionalism and credibility, I answer questions with professional care and respect for the Court.

Answering questions usually initially involves discussing my own qualifications, general information about the Battered Woman Syndrome, Post-traumatic Stress Disorder, and emotional abuse when they exist. Then, the expert is often asked to describe when/where (dates and location) she has evaluated the client and the means of evaluation. Subsequently, the expert explains the results of the evaluation.

Rather than the cooperative climate often found in psychotherapy, an attack modality, adversarial by nature, usually permeates the atmosphere in a courtroom. I discovered during my first experience as an expert witness that arguing back with a lawyer's somewhat blunt and confronting statements is not useful. I think an attorney indicated that my testimony was worthless because I had only based it on "what she (the victim) told me." I argued back that I had a great deal of experience and knew what I was talking about. This went on and on. The judge told me to stop arguing. This did not help me to establish a professional image and credibility with the jury.

Fortunately, my mistake did not harm the woman. Now, I confine my answers to brief ones with limited additional information when necessary. I would have (and have on many other occasions) answered that same question with a reply indicating that in the clinical evaluation, the diagnosis goes beyond what someone "says," to include exploring for truthfulness, examining a cluster of symptoms based on scientific research, and observing/diagnosing the individual based on many years of clinical experience.

Whatever professional qualifications are utilized, the therapist should use them with confidence while testifying based on a foundation which will stand up to criticism. Difficult questions often posed by an attorney include: "Why didn't she leave?" and "How could she have not known what was going on during the incident (the crime)?"

But the expert is just that- one who has evaluated and made a determination that adds to the understanding of the client's behavior. The client may be vulnerable, traumatized, in a state of shock and disbelief. She may have attempted to utilize the police and legal systems without success. The manner in which the expert explains abuse experiences to the jury can make a difference in the jury's understanding of the relationship between abuse and some illegal activities, ultimately impacting on the verdict (guilty or acquitted of various charges) and sentence (incarceration, probation, length of sentence, mandatory counseling, a half-way house).

This is a heavy emotional load for therapists who need to be aware of their own anxiety, concerns, and trauma. It is often useful and comforting to carry one or more sheets of paper when testifying so that the expert has access to important dates and facts. These sheets may be examined by either lawyer during the expert's testimony. The manner of the expert and the information conveyed are not the only factors in the trial. The lawyer must be effective, and there are the unfolding events that comprise the incident, as well as the victim's testimony. However, the expert can often make a difference in the victim's fate. Being professional, accurate, credible, and human are crucial skills of a therapist engaged in forensic work. With the increasing awareness of trauma sweeping the country and the world, therapists should be prepared for being asked or even subpoenaed to give court testimony regarding new clients or victims currently being seen in therapy.

Federal laws

Regarding federal laws, the expert witness needs to work closely with the attorney to understand what information is important and which is not. After the evaluation has been completed, the lawyer may ask the expert whether duress or coercion was involved in precipitating the client's illegal behavior. Coercion would include threats to destroy property, harm the victim, her family, pets, or nonfamily members, as well as threats to abandon the victim or reminders of past violent behavior on the part of the abuser (As in, "You saw me punching the dog, and I'll do the same to you and the children if you don't do this.") Duress can be offered as a possible explanation for the victim's behavior.

As has been noted, the purpose is to explore whether there is an avenue for a "downward departure" in sentencing- asking the Court to allow a lesser sentence, such as probation. Otherwise, the federal guidelines are very specific as to the length of incarceration to be considered for each type of crime.

The attorney may explain to the expert that another focus of attention involves whether there was "diminished capacity." That is, did some form of diminished emotional capacity impact on the client's behavior, presenting a potential opportunity for downward departure? The therapist must pull from the evaluation any relevant facts and decide whether such factors as the Stockholm Syndrome, Post-traumatic Stress Disorder, Battered Woman Syndrome, emotional abuse, and/or traumatic bonding are present.

I once testified in a federal court where the judge initiated a conversation with me. Sometimes federal courts tend to be more informal than state trials. For example, a woman had been physically and emotionally abused by her husband, who threatened to have his friends rape their two sons and then hang and kill them. With this in mind, she obeyed his instructions to forge someone else's signature on a check. The judge expressed his opinion that a woman who broke the law is responsible and therefore guilty. He gave an example that went something like this:

> If I robbed a bank, I would choose whether or not to go in and hold up my gun to rob the bank.

I looked at the defense lawyer to get guidance and she nodded, which I interpreted as an indication for me to go ahead and converse with the judge. The expert is an expert on the information and content, while the attorney has a decision-making role in the area of defense strategy.

I answered the judge:

> Your Honor, if a person held a gun to your child's head and said to you, 'You go in there and rob that bank or I'll shoot your child in the head,' then- your Honor- being the caring parent that I believe you must be, I believe you would have no choice.

We engaged in a back and forth discussion for a few minutes. I glanced at the defense attorney, who smiled and nodded once again, so I continued. The judge became thoughtful and silent as we looked at each other.

In this case, the lawyer had been very effective. An investigator had done beautiful work documenting the woman's past abuse- physical and emotional. The charges against the victim were dropped within a few weeks.

Part IV

Wendi: Emotional Abuse as an Antecedent to Murder

Chapter Ten

Attachment Anxiety: A Letter Regarding the Early Years

Dear Marti,

You asked me to write a letter describing my childhood. So this letter is going to be about my early years. I'm not sure I had too many of them. I felt like an adult at an early age.

When I was young, I took care of my mother a lot. She had drinking problems. She would criticize whatever I cooked. I remember cooking meals when I was six years old for my five brothers and sisters. When I was twelve, my stepfather started having sex with me. He told me, "You better not tell or your mom won't believe you." I was scared to tell Mom cause she wouldn't understand and might think I made it happen.

Even when Mom was there, she really wasn't. I mean, some problem or another occupied her mind. Perhaps a social gathering or some church event would be the center of her attention. Or she would stare out the window for a long time. When I would come to her with a problem, she always seemed too busy to be bothered. Mom would say that the problem wasn't important, give a quick solution and be off with her other business.

My two brothers were the apple of my mom and my stepfather's eyes. They could do no wrong. I was overweight and Mom said that

I was ugly. She said I'd never amount to anything. You can imagine how they all feel about the accident, when Jim died. I still can't even believe it happened.

I remember feeling scared all the time when I was a child. My stepfather would yell a lot. I would literally fold my chest and crunch my shoulders in an effort to be smaller and protect myself. The loneliness was the worst. We never discussed feelings, or we would be put down and ridiculed. My older brother was very sarcastic. So was my stepfather who came into our family when I was twelve. My dad died when I was five years old and I still miss him. He wasn't home much. He worked as a train conductor. But he was warm and loving to me. I felt very alone after he died.

My stepfather always seemed to find something to criticize about me. It seemed like no one understood me. I hated it when he made fun of me. He would say I was ugly and smelled. And he said I had sex with my boyfriend. I didn't, but my stepfather seemed to always want me to stay at home.

I caught him looking in the crack of my door when I was undressing. Maybe I was 13 years old. I hadn't realized that he was at home. He must have slipped in quietly. He usually yells a lot when he arrives home. Then he started bumping into me around the house and hugging me.

I had some nice friends growing up. But I was so afraid of being hurt. I don't think I talked much about my feelings. It seemed safer not to. My boyfriends in high school were very intellectual and not warm.

I did well with grades in high school. I never went on to college. My stepfather said I was too dumb to do well in college. Now, I take care of a family's children and clean their house. They have invited me to read their books. There is a wonderful library at their home. Both of them are teachers. I love to read and discuss books with them.

When I started dating Jim, he was really the first man I ever loved. I lived with him over weekends when I wasn't staying with the family. We had been together for ten years. I just can't believe what happened.

Jim would threaten me and keep my money. But I never minded. He said I was stupid. Jim told me that he loved me. He said my ideas were silly. I stopped telling him about my ideas. And he was jealous. Jim thought I was having an affair. I wasn't. When would I have time? Jim told me that he had followed me a few times until he made sure where I was going. I had to be sure to call my mother and friends from the family's home. Jim hated for me to use the telephone at our home.

Sometimes he was so loving, but even during those times he was critical of me. He couldn't seem to stop criticizing me, ever. I felt very small inside. He'd get angry and wouldn't talk to me, sometimes leave the house.

Since I married Jim when I was 16, I included the parts about him in my letter. I think I was a child then. Sometimes I think I'm a child now. I feel like I missed my childhood. Sometimes I look into the mirror just to remember who I am. I wonder if I'm really the person who shot Jim. I don't even remember the gun going off. I just remember him saying I didn't deserve to live and aiming the gun at me like he did once before. When he shot at me before, he hit the vase just next to me. I knew then that he could kill me when he got so mad. And he was just that mad, saying I didn't deserve to live and then I heard the shot. I didn't even know I'd done it. If I knew I would do this, I don't think I'd have wanted to survive childhood. I wish it had been me who was shot.

I had bad dreams as a child: My stepfather yelled at me and my mother ignored me in these dreams. I have nightmares now. Jim talks to me. He is threatening me in the nightmares, like he did before I shot him. And in other nightmares, asleep and during the day, I keep seeing him fall down after the shot, like it's really happening again. When I was a child and had bad dreams, I couldn't stop the sad things that happened. It's the same now. The child in me cries out that it should have been me killed, not the person I love.

With Best Regards and
Appreciation for Your Being There
For me,
Wendi

Chapter Eleven

Trauma

Shock

Wendi was stunned that the gun had "gone off," and she lost the only person she had loved. Wendi experienced trauma involving the shock and disbelief that she would have killed someone. But "they told me that I was standing over him with the gun in my hand, so I must have done it."

All physically and/or emotionally abused women are vulnerable to experiencing trauma when one perceives oneself as facing imminent death. And all therapists can encounter family violence while helping clients. Therefore, it is crucial that therapists recognize physical and/or emotional abuse and that they warn clients of the lethal potential. The victim is at risk for being killed, experiencing accidents and health problems, striking back in terror and shock, and/or becoming a victim-perpetrator.

Jim had threatened to kill Wendi. He followed her around the house for hours threatening to murder her and then threatening to kill her mother and pet dog. Jim said he'd kill her if she left the house. He had been drinking heavily. "The end of your time is here," is what Wendi most clearly remembers him repeating. There was a constant torrent of emotional abuse.

> He had beaten me before. That didn't scare me. It was all that following me around and the threats. I thought I'd die that night. And when he said he'd kill my mom and dog, I felt lost and beaten. I couldn't take anymore. I don't remember everything that happened after that. He got his gun and I thought, 'This is it.' I'm going to die.

The hospital had previous records of Wendi's broken arm, broken nose, head wounds, and a concussion. She had relayed a different story each time she went to the emergency room: "Some cans fell on my head; I fell down the stairs; I bumped into a concrete wall."

> They never asked me what happened. Jim was in the room with me each time I went to the hospital. I wish they had asked him to leave the room. I wish they had asked me what really happen – who had hurt me. Maybe he'd be alive today.

Wendi had reached out, but her shock, fear, and hopelessness impaired the cry for help. The helpers didn't hear her and reach back with understanding.

> I never called the police. Actually, I did telephone the police once from a pay phone on my way home from work. I asked them what to do about a friend of mine who was being beaten. The officer said that he wouldn't talk to me about that. He said that I should have my friend call. Once, after he broke my nose, I called for help. I snuck the telephone into the bathroom. I let the water run and called the women's shelter. I told them I had a friend in trouble with beatings. They suggested that I have her call. And they gave me good ideas about abuse.

The DSM-IV (1994) describes the Post-traumatic Stress Disorder (PTSD) as

> the development of characteristic symptoms following exposure to an extreme traumatic stressor involving direct personal experience of an event that involves actual or threatened death or serious injury, or other threat to one's physical integrity; or witnessing an event that involves death, injury, or a threat to the physical integrity of another person … (p. 424)

Examples include domestic battering, being taken hostage, and the experience of being tortured (American Psychiatric Association, 1994).

Shock-related symptoms characteristic of PTSD include flashbacks, intrusive thoughts, nightmares, psychic amnesia (also called psychogenic amnesia), avoidance of stimuli associated with the trauma, problems with concentration, a sense of a foreshortened future, psychic numbing in which there is a sense of detachment, difficulties in sleeping, hypervigilance, and distress at events or factors resembling the original trauma (DSM-IV, 1994).

It is difficult for someone experiencing shock to express the terror and horror that overwhelms her existence. The trauma that can result from emotional abuse is no less severe than the shock-related symptoms of traumatized war veterans and disaster victims. There is a sad dimension when the helping services are not responsive to this unfolding human tragedy.

A national tragedy exists in which emotionally abused women in shock, like Wendi, pass unrecognized through hospital emergency services (Loring and Smith, 1994). A dramatic increase in the recognition of battered women presenting with trauma in hospital emergency rooms has been reported following the introduction of a protocol for identifying battered women. While 5.6% of 359 female trauma patients were identified as injured in relation to battering before the introduction of the identification protocol, 30% of 412 patients were identified as having battered-related trauma injuries following the utilization of the protocol (McLeer and Anwar, 1989).

Non-leaving behavior

"Why didn't she leave?" This is an often-asked question in the legal system when emotionally abused and/or physically battered women remain in the relationship. Symonds (1975) describes a paradox in victims of crime such that

> ... overwhelming terror in a victim causes clinging, nonthinking behavior; he clings to the very person who has placed him in danger (p. 22).

Symonds uses hostage-taking as an example to point out the type of violence in which a victim stays in contact with a powerful abuser, who continues to terrorize while the victim experiences a frozen and frightened reaction. It is this immobilization that characterizes the terror of emotionally abused and/or physically battered women.

Continuous emotional abuse involving threats of harm, interwoven with loving warmth, is confusing to the victim. And, when physical abuse is present, the cycle of violence (Walker, 1984) is characterized by a build-up of tension, explosion of rage, and honeymoon period with promises of no more violence, leaving confusion and hope in its wake. There is a paradox of hope in the relationship. Both hope of the abuser's changing and hopelessness about maintaining a consistent, warm connection permeate the emotional abuse victim's life. The cycle of violence is not always present.

This emotional abuse victim is tied to the abuser by traumatic bonding: In this type of bonding, a physically battered individual experiences alternately positive, kindly responses and negative, abusive reactions (Dutton and Painter, 1981). This precipitates the traumatic component of bonding brought about by this intermittent reinforcement. For emotional abuse victims, the traumatic bonding is born of warmth interwoven amidst the continuous emotional abuse (Loring, 1994). The trauma stems from the breaking of intimate connection and the subsequent loss and grief which are a hallmark of emotional abuse. This traumatic bonding is difficult to break. Thus, abused women often remain with the abuser in the midst of others asking, "Why don't they leave?"

Manifesting symptoms

Physically battered women are viewed as having "metaphorically 'died'/disintegrated at the time of the trauma" (Niles, 1992). Symptoms of this disintegrated stated can include anxiety, depression, and/or substance abuse (Niles, 1992). In addition, nightmares and flashbacks are common among traumatized individuals (Herman, 1992). Furthermore, the trauma of battered women has resulted in such psychosomatic problems as headaches, asthma, allergies, choking, gastrointestinal problems and hyperventilation (Hilberman and Munson, 1977–78).

Emotional abuse victims experience similar symptomatology, including asthma, bladder problems, headaches, stomach aches, upper respiratory illness, flashbacks, and disintegration (Loring, 1994). Thus, it is crucial for therapists to diagnose the emotional abuse process among clients who are largely unaware of their dilemma, unable to self-identify, and suffer from a range of physical illness.

Chapter Twelve

The Therapist as an Expert Witness in State Court

Evaluation

Wendi was referred to me for a psychosocial evaluation. The lawyer explained during the referral call that she had shot and killed her husband, Jim. When we had the first interview, Wendi was incarcerated. Shortly after I received her letter and before our second interview, she was released with an ankle bracelet that monitored her whereabouts.

Visiting a client in prison often requires a letter from the lawyer which the mental health professional presents to gain entry (in addition to a driver's license and a second picture identification). The therapist's expression of concern and appropriate self-disclosing is helpful and effective when interviewing emotionally abused and/or battered women involved in committing violence. Carrying along pocket tissues is also helpful in talking with a crying, despairing victim when there is contact. A judge's order may be required.

Their trust is shattered and despair is pervasive. Hope is drowned in remorse and horror. Some small measure of healing and essential information-gathering is most effective when the therapist strives to understand their tragedy, validate their feelings, empathize with the grief and share parts of herself as a caring and nonjudgemental helper. The climate becomes one of open sharing and revelation. The richness of an evaluation is enhanced by moving in and out of questions needed for the diagnosis and allowing the client to tell her story and heartfelt feelings.

It is like the therapist takes a journey into another world and set of experiences. The deeper an understanding of the whole client that the therapist can reach, with all of the human facets of life, the better expert witness the therapist will become-whether writing a report for the lawyer to utilize during a plea bargain (when appropriate) or preparing to testify.

Therapist/evaluators need to be in touch with their own feelings about the murder and surrounding information. Some of the violent details, including possible pictures of the murdered individual and the autopsy results, can cause trauma in the therapist who reviews such documents as police and hospital records. Difficulties in sleeping and nausea, depression and anguish, are not unusual reactions for a therapist who may need to seek support from colleagues.

After an hour of sobbing in the prison visiting cell, Wendi told me,

> I wish so much that I had shot myself instead. I thought about it often. I felt so bad and ugly. How could this have happened? I love Jim. I grabbed his gun off of his desk when he threatened to kill me. Then I felt so terrified that I couldn't breathe. He kept saying that I was to die soon and then I don't remember what happened. The police said that I shot him three times. Someone called them when they saw me wandering around outside, shouting and crying. I don't remember anything until I woke up in the prison cell. I wish so badly that I had killed myself. I would rather it had been me than him. I can't sleep or eat. I have nightmares. Even when I'm awake, I see it happening again and again.

Human regret is extremely painful. It is also important to capture this deep guilt and remorse in a court testimony in order to help people understand the human dilemma of the emotionally abused and/or physically battered woman. The therapist should check out current suicidal ideation, whether the client is incarcerated or out on bond. Discovering the reasons that the woman has for going on with life is valuable and- if those reasons are not present- careful monitoring of suicidal ideation or hospitalization must be considered.

The hope for a peaceful and loving relationship, even with someone who was abusive, has been destroyed. And- paradoxically she has killed the person whom she loves. This results in intense pain, grief and sorrow.

Some women express relief at an end of the emotional torture and physical battering by the deceased partner. Most of the victims are suffocating in grief, regret and horror at their own behavior. Many women experience all of these feelings.

Possible symptoms of the Battered Woman Syndrome (Walker, 1984), the Post-traumatic Stress Disorder (DSM-IV, 1994) and patterns of ritualistic emotional abuse (Loring, 1994) should be explored, as well as possible components of the cycle of abuse (Walker, 1984). A primary goal is to evaluate whether or not the woman has experienced the Battered Woman Syndrome, Post-traumatic Stress Disorder (PTSD) or emotional abuse. If these are present and the woman believed that she was in imminent danger (Browne, 1987) at the time of the incident, the attorney may decide to use a self-defense argument.

Emotional abuse as an antecedent to murder

Wendi was physically abused prior to the murder of Jim. However, at the time of the murder, emotional abuse was present in the absence of actual physical abuse. During later discussion, Wendi described the cumulative effects of her prior sexual abuse (by her stepfather) and physical abuse by Jim. Wendi explained that having been sexually abused left her with a sense of helplessness: The question in her mind was whether she could ever escape from abuse in her life. Also, she depicted a sense of expectation since childhood following the sexual abuse: "Really bad things will happen to me." Thus, this sense of helplessness and fearful expectation were probably operating prior to the murder, as was the sense of impending physical abuse.

Wendi said that Jim's threats to kill her were terrifying prior to the incident (the shooting). He went into detail, describing her funeral and suggesting that he would kill her pet dog and bury it with her. After hearing this, Wendi began to have flashbacks to Jim's actually having punched the dog and having held a loaded gun to her head. She experienced confusion and fear, as well as a sense of a foreshortened future. She was convinced that Jim was going to kill her. Wendi lost a sense of what was happening and later was unable to remember anything beyond that point other than feeling a sense of horror. This amnesia was part of the Post-traumatic Stress Disorder (PTSD) that Wendi was experiencing. Having experienced a previous incident in which she thought Jim would kill her, this time Wendi was certain that her death was at hand and this surpassed the threshold of human endurance.

Thus, in addition to past physical and sexual abuse that set the stage for Wendi's feelings of helplessness and fear of harm, the emotional abuse in the form of threats precipitated the trauma that drove Wendi to the tragic murder. Emotional abuse victims experiencing PTSD may manifest multiple shots with a gun or slicing/jabbing motions with a knife as a result of flailing behavior characteristic of PTSD. That is, the victim throws her arms about while holding a knife or shoots a gun multiple times in sheer panic and terror, without an awareness of this behavior if experiencing amnesia.

Amnesia and depersonalization

Amnesia and depersonalization are sometimes experienced together by traumatized women who strike back at the abuser. If the trauma is severe, these women may not be able to remember pulling the trigger. "The gun went off," is common language in this situation. The terminology conveys a sense of helplessness and shock. I evaluated one women who was threatened when he affirmed that he would kill her the moment they left a restaurant.

She was carrying his gun for him in her purse. She remembered walking over to the cashier counter with him while he was muttering, "death, death," under his breath. That is the last that this individual remembers until she recalls standing over him in front of the cashier with his gun in her hand. He was on the floor, bleeding from his chest and mouth. She knelt down, held him and rocked him in her arms. He later died.

For Wendi, extensive questioning and requestioning yielded the same difficulty in remembering the actual shooting. She did not doubt that she had shot Jim, but could not recall it. Wendi was flooded with regret and thoughts about "what if" she had done something differently. This is the same self-blame that permeates a victim's life prior to the accident.

Depersonalization is frequently described by abused women who strike back at the abuser. Wendi described her feelings before, during and after the shooting:

> I felt like I was up on the ceiling watching an event unfolding. It was moving in slow motion, like in a movie. I was watching myself.

This shock reaction often involves a victim's perception of either fast-motion or slow-motion movements of herself and others during the incident.

> When trauma strikes, durational sense will change ... The event may actually be remembered in slow motion ... time appears to contract, to race faster than the clock actually moves (Terr, 1990, p. 157).

The therapist as an educator

The therapist should help others to grasp the powerful impact of emotional abuse, physical battering, helplessness, traumatic bonding, the Battered Woman Syndrome, PTSD, fear, terror generated by threats and destruction of the victim's sense of self. All of this is crucial for attorneys, juries and judges to understand. When requested by the attorney, it is important for the expert witness to write a clear report that conveys the relationship of any or all of these factors if they are present in a victim's desperation and subsequent behavior.

When testifying in court, it is important for the expert to explain these concepts in an honest and effective manner, using examples that bring home to the jurors the truthful and tragic dimensions of family violence, trauma, childhood abuse and adult revisiting of old terror.

The testimony

During jury trial selection, many attorneys instill some understanding of the trauma process by asking jurors if they or a family member have experienced family violence or some other form of trauma and trauma symptomatology. The expert witness is usually not present during the jury selection or subsequent testimony, to prevent tainting the expert testimony.

The expert must be qualified (explain her or his qualifications and have the court accept the expert status). She will be guided by the attorney while testifying in the area of her evaluation. The credibility of the expert can be crucial to the outcome of a case, as is the effectiveness of the lawyer. Some lawyers will poll a jury after the trial is over, as well as conferring with the judge. There may be feedback regarding the credibility and style of the expert witness.

Part V

Jeremy: Emotional Abuse by Parents

Chapter Thirteen

Hitting a Child with Words

A play by Jeremy Michael Massey

Spring middle school

It all started with Clyde. He's a boy. Clyde's 12 years old. He wanted to get his dad the best birthday gift ever bought in the whole city. But Clyde didn't have any money. He had an allowance, but it was used up. The allowance was five dollars a week. And Clyde got a B on his report card. The other grades were good, but the B was bad. His punishment was no allowance for four months. Also, he was grounded. He had to study every day after school. And Clyde was not allowed any phone calls for a punishment. So he could only see his friends at school. And he couldn't have any dessert for four months, too.

Clyde was very sad. But he was sad before the B. Clyde had a father named Sam. Sam wanted Clyde to get all A's. No B's ever. Sam wanted Clyde to become a doctor. A surgeon would be good. And Sam's wife, who was Clyde's mother, was sad all of the time. Clyde never knew what made his mother so sad, but she cried a lot. And Sam yelled at her and called her 'stupid.'

So Clyde figured he would earn money to buy a great gift for his dad. It would be a drill, an electric one like Sam said he wanted. But it cost over 20 dollars. How to get that much money? That was the problem. And Clyde was getting pretty tired of peanut butter sandwiches every day for lunch. He brought it from home to save lunch money. Boy, he missed those toasted cheese sandwiches and cupcakes at school!

Well, Clyde thought a lot. He just had to buy the present for his dad. He went to talk with a neighbor down the street.

"I want help," Clyde said to the neighbor. His neighbor was sweeping steps.

"I need money to buy my dad a birthday present. I never do much of anything right. I really want to get a good one."

"Well, I can't get you a job, son," the neighbor said. "You're too young."

Clyde thanked the neighbor and left. He walked to the school and found his teacher sitting at her desk. Clyde had black, curly hair. Some girls said he was cute. And his grandmother said he was very handsome. She kissed him a lot. And the teacher liked Clyde. He helped her erase blackboards. After school he carried her books sometimes out to her car. She was really nice to him. She said good things about Clyde, like he was considerate and a smart boy. No one else said that. He told her about wanting the present for his father and needing money. She said, "I'll think about it." He thanked her and left.

Clyde was sitting on the back steps of the school after he'd talked to the teacher. His head was down, and he was crying. Clyde saw someone looking at him from a window in the school. The school counselor, Mrs. Landow, came out and sat next to him.

"Hello, Clyde, what is hurting you?" she said.

He liked the way she said that. His father couldn't stand for him to cry and called him a disgusting baby for any tears. Clyde never understood why he wasn't supposed to cry. His mother drank a lot of wine and cried all the time. Ms. Landow put her arm around him and hugged him. That made Clyde cry more because it felt good. He explained the problem- no money for a good present for his father, a really great one.

"Why is it a big deal to spend money on this present?" she asked. "Could you make one?"

"No," Clyde explained to her. "My Father likes only the best. My mother says he buys the best of everything, like watches and pens and cars. He's a lawyer. We have a Mercedes. I can't make anything that good. I never do really good things for him. A great present would make him happy."

The counselor said, "So he buys expensive stuff. Happiness isn't stuff."

Clyde said, "I've never really given him anything he liked. He wasn't happy when I did yardwork or washed his car. He doesn't like me or Mom. She hangs out in her room. Cries and drinks and stuff. Lots of wine. Won't make me lunch. Or supper either sometimes. Just cries. If I do really good, get Dad his awesome present, maybe she'll be happy. And make me lunch. Dad has food in the refrigerator. But it isn't the same. Her sandwiches are good. "Clyde, my man," she'll say. "You cool, babe."

"So he doesn't dig you and she's not well wrapt- out to lunch," says Mrs. L, the counselor.

"Yeah," says Clyde.

"What do you want?" says Mrs. L.

"I want to go horseback riding with him. He likes horses. When I was little, he rode. He took me some. But he's never home now. And Mom could get with it. Like be a mom, ya know?"

Clyde cried some more. Poor Clyde. Then she said, "Hey, Clyde, maybe you could go over to old man Jones house on your street and plant some daises or something. He's gots lots of money. He'd pay you for it."

That night, Clyde gave his dad a birthday card. His birthday was the next day, but Clyde couldn't wait. Clyde made the card. It had a horse and two riders. One rider had 'Clyde' written under it. The other said, 'Dad.' And he gave his mom a hug. His dad laughed and said the horse looked like a Zebra. Then he said the Zebra looked pregnant. He said he'd never ride a pregnant horse and laughed some more. His mom said, "Oh Clyde, you messed up my hair." Clyde cried. His father yelled and said Clyde was stupid and weak. Clyde ran to his room. He wanted to be dead. A car would smush him.

Everyone who came to see him dead was sad. Clyde thought about the pills in his mother's bathroom.

Clyde called Mrs. L. and cried and told her. He said, "I wanna be dead." And she asked, "Are you for real?" He said, "Yeah. I wanna take Mom's pills."

"Please don't," she said.

"O.K., I won't," Clyde said.

A nice (and cute) police lady came to the house. She said, "I'm gonna take you away from here. To where they like kids."

Clyde said, "No, no. I don't wanna go. I just want my mom and dad to be nice to me. So make em. Why do I hafta go?"

"O.K.," says the cop, "you go to therapy tomorrow. You can stay home from school. If you go to therapy."

"Yeah, sure thing," says Clyde.

The next day they go and see this neat therapist, Mike. He talked to Clyde and his mom. Then Mike calls Clyde's dad. "You gotta come down here," says Mike. Like man, your son's gonna kill himself." Boy was he cool.

"Don't wanna miss work," says Clyde's dad. "Clyde's a jerk. Spoiled and dumb."

"No," says Mike. "You hurt him bad with your yelling and dumb-names for him." So Clyde's dad comes to Mike's office.

Clyde's dad starts smarting off to Mike, "Get a grip. Get a life. It's my stupid son."

"Hello. Wake up, you," says Mike. He goes, "Knock, knock," to Clyde's dad. "hello, is anybody in there?" says Mike.

Clyde says, "You do hurt me Dad. It's like when my finger got caught in the car door. Man it hurt. But it stopped. You don't stop, Dad. Not ever."

So that's all. Mike made Clyde's mom go to the hospital. She stopped drinking. His dad got straight. And they went on their horseback ride. And Clyde's dad liked Clyde. You shouldn't call a kid stupid or they really will be. Or they'll be dead.

Chapter Fourteen

Emotional Abuse of Children: A Theoretical Perspective

CLYDE is Jeremy's alter ego- the symbol of Jeremy's own suffering. Sad and lonely himself, Jeremy described Clyde's emotional and physical abandonment and neglect by his mother. He also depicted Clyde's father emotionally abusing Clyde who felt demeaned and diminished. Suicidal ideation is common among emotionally abused children and adolescents. It is their translation of the ultimate emotional abuse message: You plus your ideas, feelings and perceptions are either worthless or do not exist.

In *The Psychologically Battered Child*, Garbarino, Guttmann and Seeley (1989) examine different forms of emotional abuse toward children. This abuse is placed in both a systems and a developmental perspective. Systemically, the child is viewed in the context of not only the family, but also the larger society with its values, institutions and intervention programs. From a developmental perspective, various ages and stages are noted as impacting on the severity and type of harm caused by abuse. That is,

> Development is emergent social competence, a growing sense of 'self in the world' that is based in the day-to-day realities of ever wider spheres of social performance. Retaining this developmental focus, we ... specify the behaviors that constitute rejecting,

> terrorizing, ignoring, corrupting and isolating in each of the major stages in the first eighteen years of life: infancy (birth to age two), early childhood (ages two to five), school age (five to eleven) and adolescence (eleven to eighteen). Each of these periods has its own particular developmental issues and corresponding social correlates. Similarly, we recognize the need to deal with degrees of severity: mild, moderate and severe (p. 22).

In the area of emotional abuse toward children, the degree of severity is determined by an interplay of developmental stages, impairment of functioning and impact on individual and social growth:

> We describe as "mild" those instances of psychological maltreatment that create the risk of limited psychic damage confined to one aspect of functioning (such as lack of confidence in public settings); "moderate" refers to instances of maltreatment that may prevent a child from achieving minimal success in important settings (for instance, at school); the label "severe" refers to instances of maltreatment that will, in all likelihood, cause children to be crippled in one or more of life's primary settings-work, love and play (p. 22–23).

The definition of maltreatment and five primary forms of abuse are couched in a psychosocial conceptual framework that captures the impact of abuse on a child and his or her social development, as well as the actual abusive behavior by an adult:

> In our definition, psychological maltreatment is a concerted attack by an adult on a child's development of self and social competence, a *pattern* (italicized in text) of psychically destructive behavior and it takes five forms:
>
> *Rejecting* (the adult refuses to acknowledge the child's worth and the legitimacy of the child's needs).
>
> *Isolating* (the adult cuts the child off from normal social experiences, prevents the child from forming friendships and makes the child believe that he or she is alone in the world).
>
> *Terrorizing* (the adult verbally assaults the child, creates a climate of fear, bullies and frightens the child and makes the child believe that the world is capricious and hostile).

> *Ignoring* (the adult deprives the child of essential stimulation and responsiveness, stifling emotional growth and intellectual development).
>
> *Corrupting* (the adult "mis-socializes" the child, stimulates the child to engage in destructive antisocial behavior, reinforces that deviance and makes the child unfit for normal social experience).

Jeremy, a twelve year old child with sandy brown hair and large brown eyes, is rejected and ignored by his mother, who does not provide consistent care for him. She rarely cooks meals or fixes food for Jeremy. Sometimes, there is not enough food in the refrigerator for him to make lunch for himself. He eats nuts until his father comes home and goes out to get groceries. Or he makes a peanut butter sandwich for his lunch.

Jeremy explained to his therapist a game he plays: Jeremy pretends that he is a squirrel named "Ymerej" (backwards spelling of his name). According to Jeremy, Ymerej has a mother who loves him very much but sometimes becomes overcome by the paint fumes of the house where their nest rests upon a roof. The owner of the house likes to change the house color frequently, thus the mother's fume-reaction of sleepiness and inability to collect nuts for the young ones is inevitable from time to time.

The rejection experienced by Jeremy involves his mother's inability to maintain the attachment with him. She struggles with substance abuse and depression in the context of her own emotional abuse by her husband. Jeremy described to his therapist frequent dreams involving abandonment of both himself and baby animals. Terrified that his parents will "send me away somewhere because I don't do things right," Jeremy experiences the rejection as due to his own inadequacies, rather than his mother's problems or his father's excessive expectations.

> I feel lost. Like I'm a dog and my owners moved away. They forgot to take me. Dad gives me dirty looks. He won't talk to me if I mess up. He just yells and yells at me. Said I'd be better off dead. Calls me stupid and dummy a lot. Dad can't stand for me to hang with my friends. And they make good grades. He makes me stay in my room for no reason. Won't let me use the phone. Says I'm useless, a jerk. Sometimes I cry and throw up.

> Just cause I'm sad, ya know? If I throw up, he says I'm disgusting. Says maybe he'll break my neck. It scares me. Mom just cries. Shut up in her room. Like a dead lady. I miss her. I am pretty dumb.

Jeremy is terrorized by his father, resulting in Jeremy's fear and shame even while making maximum effort for a child of his age. His grades are A's with a rare B. His dad's threats to break Jeremy's neck are terroristic and frightening to him. And his father attempts to keep Jeremy away from friends and his aunt, who is supportive to him. This isolates Jeremy.

Based on the model suggested by Garbarino, Guttmann and Seeley (1989), the constant criticism that Jeremy's father exposes him to, as well as the unrealistic demands to constantly excel, are manifestations of terrorism. Moreover, Jeremy is experiencing rejection in that the father is defining Jeremy as a continual failure. And Jeremy feels ignored and rejected by his mother, who is depressed and abusing alcohol.

Overt emotional abuse

Jeremy is yelled at, degraded through such labels as "stupid" and "worthless," not cared for with consistent meals, punished for normal physical reactions like vomiting, and subjected to continual criticism. Jeremy is isolated from others when forced to stay inside, rather than being allowed to play with friends or attend social functions.

Covert emotional abuse

At the same time, Jeremy experiences ongoing emotional abuse that is subtle, yet powerful in its impact on his development. He struggles with **discounts** when his father interrupts him and insists that Jeremy's ideas, feelings and perceptions are not important. In addition, **negation** is evident when Jeremy's expressed opinion or feeling is followed by his father's statement that Jeremy does not feel this way. His father often comments that there is "no such idea" as one expressed by his son.

> I told dad, 'I wanta be a teacher. They help people to learn.' Dad said, 'No man, you don't feel that way cause no one wants to be a teacher.' He said, 'what you want doesn't count you ugly dumbo.' I got messed up in my head. Like I couldn't think right. Just kept remembering what he said all day. Kept in my mind his words. I wasn't sure what I wanted to be anymore.

Jeremy is blamed for a multitude of events whenever his father feels anxious and pressured at work. When handling a difficult legal case, Jeremy's father, who is an attorney, is continuously critical of Jeremy's behavior. Even under normal circumstances, his irritation and impatience become translated into volatile anger at Jeremy's age-appropriate behavior. This **projection** involves a perception of the other as causing one's own feelings. At the same time, Jeremy's father used subtle labeling to cast negative connotations on much of Jeremy's behavior. The **negative labeling** included his father shaking his head and sighing, then

> giving me dirty looks and saying, 'Oh Jeremy.' Man, he'd be so disgusted with me. I always cover my mouth when I'd sneeze. But he yells that who wants my crummy germs. It got so he'd just look at me real disgusted. I'd get sick to my stomach. When I said, 'Dad, are you mad?' He'd say, 'No, man.' I thought it was all in my head. Like I was disgusting.

Here the father negatively labeled Jeremy as disgusting, then **denied** this when asked by Jeremy. This projection, discounting, negative labeling and negation are all mechanisms of emotional abuse toward children, as well as adults.

Covert threats to abandon by both his father and mother terrified Jeremy:

> Dad sometimes went away for a few days. When he'd get back home, he'd tell me it was to teach Mom and me a lesson. We should be glad for all he does. I get scared if he goes to the front hall closet when it's not time for him to go to work. If I forget to clean my room or feed the dog, or something, he'll cough and start going to the closet. I'll say, 'what did I do?' He'll just shrug his shoulders. I try to figure it out and ask him 'did I mess

> this up, or that?' I try real hard cause I'm scared he'll go away. But maybe that'd be good. Cause he really makes me sad.

The covert aspect of abuse involves Jeremy's dad moving toward the closet as if to leave. His father also repeatedly said, "Oh, acting that way again, are we?" Jeremy would ask how he was behaving and try to improve. He was particularly terrorized when his father would say

> 'Oh, acting that way again, are we?' That's when he's gonna walk to the closet and maybe leave. He goes 'I'm leaving cause you are so bad. I'm tired of you.' Once I asked Dad if that was what he meant. He said, 'I get real tired of you.'

Covert emotional abuse has a powerful impact on children. It can lead to confusion and fragmentation of the self. Suicidal ideation is common among emotionally abused children who are traumatized by emotional assaults, especially when the adults deny their abuse to the children. Jeremy's mother insisted to Jeremy that she loved him and always would take good care of him. He then became confused when she would retire into her locked room for long periods of time. While there was always food in the house, Jeremy would go for periods of time without a hot, cooked meal.

As with emotionally abused adults, his sadness and confusion were expressed in somatic metaphors. Jeremy experienced somatic problems like asthma, stomach aches, headaches and upper respiratory illnesses. Jeremy was diagnosed several times with bronchitis.

> My voice would go away. I could hardly talk. Really hoarse. So what's the difference? No one listened to me anyway.

The mechanisms and impact of emotional abuse toward children are the same as emotional abuse toward adults. Sadness and loneliness among emotionally abused children is profound. They feel unconnected to caring others. Some are able to connect with meaningful people in their environment, like a teacher or counselor. Those fortunate children feel some small sense of hope amidst the despair and hopelessness of emotional abuse. Even with a small degree of hope, Jeremy often felt deeply sad and lost:

> I feel all alone. Like in a big forest. I'm screaming but no one hears. I dream I'm falling down a well and can't hold on. No

> one's there. Can't hold slippery well sides. Down I go. And I hurt inside. Just feel bad. I'm so lonely I want to die. I'm so scared I'll take my mom's pills. She's gotta lot of them. If I were dead, I wouldn't hurt so much. Maybe. But Mrs. L. likes me. Says I'm cool.

Jeremy told the counselor Mrs. L. about his dad's yelling and accusations, saying that being called 'dumb' and 'worthless' was very painful. But Jeremy explained that the covert threats of his dad to abandon him and his mom's "being so cold to me, like snow in summertime" hurt him the most. Jeremy described the pain

> when Dad turned on TV real loud and I'm talking to him. Like I'm not there.

Jeremy told his therapist that there was no physical or sexual abuse.

When emotionally abused during an evening, Jeremy has difficulty concentrating in school the next day. He describes intrusive thoughts and flashbacks.

> I could hear Dad saying, 'you're worthless.' And 'you're better off in a foster home.' In my head, like I really heard him. Louder than the math teacher saying math stuff in class. That's why I got the B.

For some children, feelings of death are emotional ones. That is, the child reports a sense of "deadness" or "lifelessness" so that excitement, hope, trust and connections with others feel blunted and deflated. Jeremy felt small and hopeless,

> like a squashed mouse who squeaked sad-like

Sibling abuse

Jeremy had no sisters or brothers. But when sibling emotional abuse occurs, the same dynamics operate to prevent growth of confidence and hope in a child. One woman, Jerie, reported hearing critical remarks made by her sister when she (Jerie) was a child. Continuing into adult life, these negative and critical remarks haunted her and felt true, damaging her self-image (Wiehe, 1991).

The impact of emotional abuse

The physical and sexual abuse of children has been a primary focus in our society. However, emotional abuse is a dangerous and insidious process that erodes the confidence, abilities and sense of self among children. Rather than casting emotional abuse as an ancillary issue, subordinate to other forms of abuse and neglect, we should place it as a centerpiece of efforts to understand family functioning and to protect children.

> In almost all cases, it is the psychosocial consequences of an act that defined that act as abusive. This is true of physical abuse (consider, for example, the meaning to a child of an injury inflicted by a parent in rage compared with the same injury inflicted by accident in the course of an athletic event … it is also true of sexual abuse (since sexual acts have little or no intrinsic meaning apart from their social psychological connotations-as the incredible variety of norms regarding sexual activity in childhood and adolescence across cultures suggests) (Garbarino, Guttmann and Seeley, p. 7).

Sexual abuse creates tremendous harm and damage for the child, as does physical abuse. The plea here is for recognition of the profound impact of emotional abuse as it occurs alone or with other severe abuse.

Chapter Fifteen

Intervening with an Emotionally Abused Child

INTERVENTION with emotionally abused children is a multilevel task that should include individual work with the child, family support and change, extended family involvement and community integration. The child must be helped in reconnecting with his or her own destroyed sense of self, helped to experience safety and security within the family and extended family systems and supported in connecting with valuable community resources. Individual therapy, alone, is not sufficient to facilitate healing and on-going growth in an emotionally abused child.

Reporting of emotional abuse to state child protective agencies is appropriate. In Jeremy's case, the therapist's call to the state child protective agency resulted in a judgement by an agency staff member that Jeremy's emotional abuse was not severe enough to warrant an investigation.

Identifying emotional abuse

Emotional abuse is frequently missed in evaluating children. Thus, the first step in intervention is the evaluation of children for emotional abuse. This evaluation should include questions and observations not only regarding the inner psyche, but also a clear mapping of the presence of abuse in external connections. In emotional abuse, the child is degraded and deprived of warm, available attachment. Symptoms include the child's self-fragmentation, loneliness and fearfulness.

The method of posing therapeutic questions depends on the age and skills of the child, as well as the therapist's style. With young children two, three, or four years old, a therapist may utilize play therapy as the primary means of evaluation. Some family therapists prefer to see the family together.

But the therapist should, if seeing the whole family, provide a safe time and place for the child to individually communicate her or his pain, its source and the impact on development and functioning. The technique is less important than the perspective- a quest for abusive symptomatology and climate. This type of screening should be available for all young people evaluated for school, family, or individual problems.

Somatic symptoms

As illustrated by Jeremy, emotionally abused children often have somatic symptomatology as a metaphor for the abuse. Stomach-aches can symbolize the sickening feeling of being punched with words. Upper respiratory illness may signify loss of voice as a result of discounting and negation. Or it can symbolize feelings of suffocation from criticisms and put-downs. Headaches or aching of other body parts often involve the aching pain of abuse and the tenseness associated with emotional violation. Bladder difficulty for girls (like frequent urination) can be a metaphor for confusion and tension regarding holding in feelings and letting them out, along with the fear of being punished or humiliated.

There are multiple possibilities to utilize when evaluating somatic suffering of children. Some useful questions to ask the child include:

1) When do you feel that pain?
2) When was the last time you experienced it and the time before that?
3) What was going on during these two times: Who were you around; what was said to you?

4) What makes you feel better?
5) What do you do to avoid this pain?

It is often helpful for the child to be helped in understanding the connection between a somatic problem and its metaphor, as in bronchitis and the loss of self or voice. Depending on the age of the child, these connections can be gained through play therapy, insight-directed discussions and/or exposure to meaningful community resources that provide positive regard and role models for the child.

Other physical symptomatology should be explored, like shrinking behavior (hunching the shoulders forward or sliding down in a chair when the abuser is speaking), wincing and constricted and/or restrained actions.

During shrinking behavior, a child literally folds up or physically withdraws from the painful stimuli. Jeremy described moving his shoulders toward the middle of his body and hanging his head, in addition to holding his arms over his stomach.

> I had a turtle. It crawled inside. Kind of folded up. I do that. Like when he yells at me. Or if Mom won't hug me. I make a ball. Like a shell in front, So I don't get hurt.

Wincing as if struck, an emotionally abused child is hypervigilant to hurtful words, abandonment, discounting, negation, negative labeling and projection. For the child, as with an adult, the emotional harm is painful like physical slapping and beating. Humiliation and degradation punch at the self-image and self-esteem of a child.

Many emotionally abused children report and can be observed engaging in obsessive-compulsive-like constricted behavior. They are physically stiff or rigid in their behavior. Some of these children take longer to complete tests and homework and many perseverate to complete household tasks in a perfectionistic manner. Concerned about criticism and shame, the child struggles to avoid this humiliation through cautious behavior or stunted action. Often confused about which feelings are acceptable, the child hides many emotions and appears restrained, lacking in spontaneity.

However, the emotionally abused child cannot avoid abuse because the rage of the abuser comes from within and is only triggered by, not a direct result of, the victim's behavior. Thus, the constriction and restrained behavior do not succeed in their intended purpose- safety from emotional abuse. This leads to profound sadness and loneliness on the part of a child. The grief involved in giving up the struggle for ongoing, consistent, warm, nonabusive connection with an abuser is a crucial area for therapeutic intervention.

The child's coming to grips with the limits of an abuser is very important. In addition to the therapist's assisting the abuser with connection or making a referral for the abuser to increase parenting skills, broadening the child's opportunities for connections with others is essential. If the abuser appears to be limited in ability to grow in connection with the child, then all of the abuser's capacity should be utilized in respect to connection with the decreased abuse of the child. Then other resources must also be used, like growth in the advocacy and connection of the remaining parent, bringing in other family members (aunts, uncles, siblings, cousins, grandparents) to add connection and support, and enhancing community advocacy. Community ties are crucial, such as "Big Brothers," the "YMCA," "YWCA," Boy and Girl Scouts. The availability and responsiveness of empathic people are crucial to counter the despair, anguish and pain of striving to connect with an unconnectable individual-an abuser whose energy and rage circles her or his own needs with little sensitivity to the needs or individuality of others.

> In my own clinical experience, abusive parents often show a bewildering lack of remorse and failure to feel the child's pain (Krugman, 1987, p. 133).

Intervention in the constriction and other manifestations of emotional abuse includes clarifying for the child the origins of wincing, constriction and shrinking behavior. Decrease in self-blame and enhanced self-esteem can be outgrowths of this kind of understanding tied to accomplishments in the community.

Trauma symptomatology

Intrusive thoughts (American Psychiatric Association, 1994) and confusion are common among emotionally abused children and adolescents, just as these symptoms occur with emotionally abused adults. Difficulty in concentration is usual. In addition, emotionally abused children often experience flashbacks in which they relive the abusive attack (American Psychiatric Association, 1994). Jeremy described flashbacks during school. These are either major or minor flashbacks (Loring, 1994). In major flashbacks the child is aware of her surroundings and cognizant that voices or images are not actually occurring in the present, versus hallucinations or delusions. Yet, the child staring off into space or exhibiting discomfort for a period of time re-experiences the actual abusive incident as well as the trauma associated with it.

During minor flashbacks, a momentary traumatic memory reoccurs as if it is happening in the present, with all of the original terror, sadness and loneliness. The child briefly stares ahead with a blank appearance, seems distracted, or exhibits anxiety while describing abuse. In response to the therapist's question, a child experiencing flashbacks is able to identify the alive, present and terrifying nature of the flashback.

Other traumatic symptoms are observed in emotionally abused children, such as sleeping problems, eating disorders, high anxiety and depression. There is disintegration of the self with terror associated with loss of sense of self. Hypervigilance is also present. As with other trauma victims, the child is often withdrawn and frightened of experiences that remind her of the trauma, such as attempts to succeed at school or other similar tasks for a child belittled and demeaned in the area of mastery and achievement.

Stealing and lying are common among young abuse victims, more so than with emotionally abused adults. Jeremy stole pencils from his teacher's desk and food from the other children's lunch bags. He explained that

> I don't know why. Just felt good, like when I fill up a bucket with sand. Then it's not so empty. I felt bad for doing it.

The lying may be an attempt to avoid punishment that is overly strict and based on unrealistic expectations.

Because the child is learning that it isn't safe to trust others to respond in a respectful and accepting way, intimacy is either avoided or sought in a source that is more trustworthy and warm. A pet, a neighbor, a school teacher or counselor can make a significant difference in the life of a young emotional abuse victim. Experience with caring, acceptance and encouragement can prevent learning a generalization that no one is trustworthy that everyone will hurt you in closeness.

It is not safe for a young emotional abuse victim to express direct anger. The abuse would escalate. Thus, anger is usually internalized and results in self-mutilation, depression and low self-esteem. Jeremy pulled off his fingernails and toenails.

Attachment anxiety (Bowlby, 1988) leads to clinging on the part of young emotional abuse victims. Yet, that clinging to nonnurturing figures often leads to further abuse in the form of discounting, rejection and abandonment. Jeremy's father threatened to send him to a foster home if he whined or asked for attention and his mother would lock herself up in her room if Jeremy cried or complained. Clinging can take many forms, such as complaining, continual futile attempts to please, attempting to convince the abuser of one's worth or intentions, verbally defending against emotional attacks when one's behavior is criticized, physically holding onto or trying to hug, whining, attempted (or successful) injuries to obtain sympathy, etc.

This clinging or anxious attachment is a normal reaction to an abnormal lack of nurturing, empathy and other types of support. It is also a desperate attempt to prevent fragmentation of the self, which leaves the terrified victim confused, profoundly lonely and sad, self-destructive with internalized anger and desperation. Many of these victims are emotionally unconnected to extended family members, a close family member, a community person, or resources in the community providing nurturing and support. Their desperation can result in substance abuse, eating disorders, depression, run-aways and/or juvenile delinquency.

Intervention with clinging emotionally abused children should be aimed at connection development on numerous levels. These levels include environmental, community, family and the child's sense of self.

Environmental, community and family interventions

Emotionally abusive families are noted for economic/vocational stresses and a family style characterized by isolation of the child, excessive expectations and harshness, marital discord and possible sibling abuse, according to Garbarino, Guttmann and Seeley (1989). These authors review literature that portray emotionally abusive parents as former victims of abuse who did not have adequate parental models and have not mastered basic parenting skills. Isolation of the family in the community is characteristic of the emotional abuse process. Furthermore, the impact of this abuse on infants, children and adolescents is marked by clinging, feeling unwanted and unloved, as well as possible withdrawal and/or striking out.

Garbarino, Guttmann and Seeley (1989) suggest a wide range of interventions, including the use of community clubs, like Big Sisters and Big Brothers and other volunteers to model parenting skills to at-risk parents. Also suggested are a child protection agency (if necessary) and referral of parents to stress-reducing agencies to help with financial and vocational problems. Both family therapy and marital counseling are explored, as is training the parents in effective child-parent interaction. These authors utilize an ecological perspective to include the whole scope of intervention strategies.

This larger view of the problem is important and therapists unfamiliar with community resources should utilize a United Way Helpline, attend training sessions and/or consult with colleagues to include all relevant resources in helping an emotionally abused child. The larger scope of helping is crucial, since individual therapy is not sufficient to help a young emotional abuse victim move toward becoming a survivor. There are simply too many negative and destructive forces crushing the young person for an hour of therapy each week to have a sustaining impact on the abusive stimuli and resulting unraveling of the self.

Intervening with the child's sense of self

The rebuilding of a diminished or destroyed sense of self in a child must take place in an atmosphere of trust and empathy. Depending on the therapist's skills and treatment methods and considering the age and developmental level of the child, the therapeutic format can involve any number of modalities. These modalities include play therapy, activity therapy, traditional therapeutic interviews, and specific skill-development methods like social skills training

(Hops, 1982) and constructive conflict management (Stocking and Arezzzo, 1979).

External reintegration

I worked with Jeremy by combining activity therapy and traditional therapeutic interviews (lasting one hour and a half weekly). In addition, Jeremy was encouraged to continue talking with the school counselor. The teacher who was attached to Jeremy was supported in obtaining his parents' permission for Jeremy to assist in planting indoor and outside plants at the school. Both parents agreed to this plan. Jeremy gained a great deal of self-confidence from his work and discussions with these two adults.

In addition, Jeremy loved crafts and acting, so I encouraged his parents to enroll him in a local theater that was planning a children's play. A volunteer interested in children provided transportation for him. During the try-outs, Jeremy was cast in a starring role and performed so well during the play that applause for him after each performance was thunderous. He asked his father for speech lessons, explaining that these lessons would help plan for a future career in either law or the theater. His father, impressed with Jeremy's assertiveness and apparent talent, agreed to pay for and provide transportation to weekly lessons. When involved in court, his father arranged for a secretary to accompany his son. Jeremy enjoyed the transportation time with his father.

During periodic check-ups with the whole family, I confronted the father with each incident of emotional abuse in my presence and asked his mother to hug Jeremy and praise him for his perseverance and, as she put it, "just plain wonderful humanness" of Jeremy.

Weekly sessions with Jeremy often involved activities in which we attempted one new adventure after another. Jeremy was responsible for coming up with the plans and for calling ahead and making reservations. He developed a sense of confidence in himself and a trust that I would never criticize or attack him for his efforts, even when he made a mistake or wasn't able to follow his directions and find our activity site. These activities included roller and ice skating, as well as walks in a botanical garden.

> I use to be scared of making mistakes. And I'd call myself 'dumbo.' And turtle up in a ball. And get stomach-aches. Now my shell is off. Like I'm flying.

I reported activities to Jeremy's mother and father, while giving them updates on Jeremy's progress and requesting their input. While Jeremy's father refused to take parenting classes, he was willing to spend a double interview with me (2 hours) discussing various ways to guide Jeremy. Part of that time, he talked about his childhood when he was beaten by his father and abandoned by his mother (at age six). He was unwilling to seek counseling on his own, but agreed to encourage his wife to attend AA meetings.

Jeremy's mother was initially willing to seek counseling and attend AA. She then dropped out of therapy (after three months), because "it makes me sad." No amount of encouragement by me convinced her to return to therapy, so I asked her to meet with me once a month to discuss Jeremy's progress. During one meeting, I encouraged her to enter an in-patient detoxification program and she spent four weeks hospitalized. Jeremy's aunt from out of town come to stay with him, which he greatly enjoyed. I met with the whole family once a week and with Jeremy biweekly (one activity and an interview session) during her hospitalization. Following her hospitalization, his mother participated in an aftercare group meeting each week. In my weekly meetings with Jeremy's mother, I modeled parenting and communication skills. Humor, positive suggestions and self-disclosure were used.

She enjoyed reading and I helped her enroll in a college course (english literature). She passed with an "A" and decided to finish college. We agreed that she needed to attend AA meetings in order to achieve this goal of finishing college and remaining sober (both of which she accomplished). During monthly individual meetings with me, she revealed past physical and sexual abuse. After several months, she agreed to weekly therapy sessions. She was attending AA three times a week.

After Jeremy's mother was discharged from the hospital, we returned to meeting once a week. Before leaving for an activity, Jeremy and I had "quiet and thinking time" during which we discussed events, feelings, hopes and ideas he had experienced during the week. When he discussed his father's occasional yelling, he had minor flashbacks. We engaged in 'retrospective recall' in which he drank some soda and relaxed physically while discussing his fears. This often resulted in a minor flashback. When his mind was empty and during the silence, he experienced additional minor flashbacks while describing past emotional abuse.

Reintegration occurs as the memories, intrusive thoughts and flashbacks are re-experienced in a safe and validating therapeutic setting. Experienced with all of the original terror, these thoughts and images lose their fear and strangling terror, becoming integrated memories that are understood and given new meaning.

We talked about the sadness and loneliness that Jeremy felt. I encouraged him to spend more time with other children. When he became a star in the play and began talking more with others, they called him at home and asked him to parties. While he was shy, he would act out characters at the parties, like famous adults or animals. Jeremy would wind up being a hit at each party. Two girls decided to pursue him and Jeremy did not choose between them because he enjoyed their telephone calls and attention so much. His father was quite proud of Jeremy's growing popularity, describing his son as "a chip off the old block."

The yelling and rejection by his father and the abandonment by his mother decreased. Jeremy and I worked on identification of and disattachment from abuse when his parents were inappropriate. I asked for and received permission from the parents, granting Jeremy sanction- when he felt abused- to excuse himself and go up to the attic where we had rigged up a theater with a stage. His mother and father went with him and helped pick out some books for him to keep in the attic and read from during disattachment periods. Jeremy expressed feeling more hopeful.

> I'm not so much mixed up in my head. Cool. Not much Mom getting sad and going away. And I go stage-it and act away. Maybe ask Bobby or Ted over. Awesome. We do plays.

Validation comes to Jeremy from me, the school counselor, his teacher, many others for his acting and from his own self-praise regarding changes and growth. Disattachment assists in his internal reintegration from the initial confusion and depression resulting from his parents' abusive behavior. This experience helps with external reintegration in which Jeremy establishes multi-connections with community, resources, peers, adults and a craft (acting) which he loves. Thus, both external and internal reintegration are crucial.

Internal reintegration

Internally, the sense of self in an emotionally abused child is greatly diminished or even destroyed. These victims do not experience their own qualities as unique and valuable. Neither can they escape from confusion, sadness and profound loneliness resulting from the emotional abuse process. Their body image is damaged: They feel unattractive and unwanted in reaction to the degradation and humiliation experienced in the abusive relationship. They are disconnected from their own sense of self.

This victim sharply experiences self-disconnection during negation, discounting, projection and denial. The victim's own boundaries, feelings and ideas are unclear in the midst of emotional assault. When unaware of the existence and violent component of covert emotional abuse, the victim suffers from depression and trauma. Self-mutilation and suicidal ideation are a means of experiencing a sense of self.

The therapist working with an emotionally abused child must help with self-reconnection. Being there as a secure base for the child, a therapist validates feelings and ideas of the young victim. Furthermore, the therapist reflects admiration, respect and caring for the child while inviting the young survivor to view the self in a more positive light. Activities that enhance the child's self-image and sense of accomplishment are very important. Analysis with the child of the growth and development experienced by the child is a crucial aspect of 1) therapy and 2) the child's evolving self-validation.

Young victims need help in identifying each cluster of their qualities, like "friendly," "polite," "brave," etc. This can be done through discussion with the therapist, or the child may be able to write or draw each characteristic. The therapist assists in the child's learning about her qualities, as well as naming them and imagining each interacting with the others in such processes as decision-making and problem-solving. Jeremy was asked to consult with the qualities he had named "Jeremy-the-Brave" (who keeps trying to succeed), "Jeremy-all-alone" (the part of him that feels profoundly lonely and misunderstood), "Jeremy-and-the-good-guys" (his efforts at connecting with encouraging and supportive people).

> You know, 'Jeremy-the-brave'(JB) and me go to the attic when Dad yells. 'Awesome kid, it's star time," that's what JB says. I keep the me-parts secret. It's a no-brainer. So no one puts me down, like Dad.

While this strategy is not useful for a client experiencing multiple personality disorder, it is helpful in creating a sense of self and identity in many emotionally abused children. The goal also involves increasing cohesion in a victim vulnerable to disintegration during emotional abuse. Thus, there is a cohesive entity to which the child can connect- his own growing sense of self that is unfolding and discovering a direction.

As the trust grows between the therapist and the child, retrospective recall continues to be useful in promoting safe recall of traumatic abusive incidents. Inviting the child to relax and reminisce about past and current abuse, as well as giving permission to stop if it becomes too painful, the therapist validates the terror of flashbacks as they are experienced by the victim. Intrusive thoughts, too, are validated. In addition, the young victim is coached in disattachment from internalized abuse (flashbacks and intrusive thoughts). Jeremy went upstairs to act and write if his own intrusive thoughts led to fear and depression.

This self-disattachment is achieved by replacing as quickly as possible an alternative connection for the abusive memory, intrusive thought and/or flashback. The connection should be meaningful and fulfilling, whether it is a thought, person, hobby, or a cause. Induction of flashbacks allows the victim to confront the terror and sadness of past and current abuse, as portrayed in the flashback, in the presence of a safe and nurturing figure. Moreover, the victim moves toward becoming a survivor by learning to be self-nurturing during disattachment from abuse in the form of flashbacks and intrusive thoughts. Disattachment from these intrusive elements gives the child a sense of being able to survive, in spite of the reoccurring pain. Children can only move toward becoming a survivor when they encounter and master the fear generated by abuse.

The 'reconstituted connectional experiences' for the child emotional abuse survivor include connecting in a caring way with himself as well with a therapist, teacher, coach, director, big brother and even parents as they decrease the abusive behavior. As described by Judy Herman (1992), victims can move toward becoming survivors by seeing a larger meaning for their suffering. As the children's pain decreases, an important part of therapeutic intervention involves helping them view their place in the world while considering what meaning their past experiences may have. Although his kind of decision may change with time, it is very satisfying for a child to recognize himself as a survivor and develop a vision of his worldview and role in the universe. Jeremy found this a moving experience.

> I'm not crying now cause I hurt. I'm crying cause I want other kids to be happy like me. I want to help hurting kids write a play. Awesome.

Part VI

Barbara Anne: Elder Emotional Abuse

Chapter Sixteen

A Telephone Call to The Holiday Hotline

"HELLO, my name is Barbara Anne and I saw you on television with your hotline. You look like you care about people. So I'm calling to talk with you. But I feel ashamed for being so sad and lonely. The lady who the television reporter interviewed from your hotline said Christmas is a hard time of year for some people. I'm one of those people. During Christmas, I miss my daughter. She was 43 when she died of breast cancer last year just after Christmas. And my husband died three years ago. I miss them both so much. They were the center of my life, my real joy. Not that I don't love my grandson and son-in-law, but they're so busy I rarely see them, even though we live a few blocks away.

And my grandson has a drug problem- crack, you know. His eyes get real big and he stares off into space. Gives me the creeps. And he thinks I don't notice when things are missing- my little portable television and my telephone, you know, one of those phones you carry around from one room to another. Whenever he comes over, maybe once a month or so, something leaves with him. I asked him last time about whether he'd seen my little portable television that my husband had given me and he shouted that I was senile and probably lost it. Boy, did that hurt my feelings! I'm 77 and don't walk with the stride I used to. That's true. But I still walk around the block two or three times a day.

And I don't have anyone to play with, but I go out to the driveway in back of my house and hit a tennis ball against the bricks of the garage every day, rain or shine, even if I have to wear gloves. I drive to the grocery in the daytime and the cleaners. I even keep my own doctor's appointments. I don't want to be a burden to anyone. Actually, I'm in very good health. Just a little high blood pressure and some arthritis. But I take my blood pressure medicine regularly, eat a banana for potassium every day (whether I'm hungry or not) and walk and hit the tennis ball a heap.

You know what it's like to get old? I wake up at night a lot to go the bathroom. But, if I can't get back to sleep, my doctor said to sip on some sherry.

'You'll make a sop out of me, with all this sipping,' I said to him. He laughed when I asked how he expected me to hit a tennis ball on a full glass of sherry. One of my friends (the only one living anymore- boy, it's lonely getting old), anyway, this friend takes medicine to wake up, to go to sleep, to increase her appetite, to keep potassium up, to keep blood pressure down, a diuretic and more. I mean the poor woman takes 18 pills twice a day and can barely keep them straight. Don't you think I'm pretty healthy and lucky?

Thank you for asking. No, I don't think I have a drinking problem, but I know some older people do. No, I don't quite finish a bottle of sherry every two weeks. Sometimes a bottle lasts for three weeks.

No, I don't see my son-in-law often. He brings me chocolate candies once a month. Funny, poor boy thinks I'm hungry for candy. I'm hungry all right. But for company and caring. I've never been one to get out much.

What do I like to do? Well, I enjoy poetry. I majored in english at college. With my teaching degree, I preferred to teach english in high school and did for many years. But I retired long ago. I use to volunteer to teach people to read. Then I got too old.

No, the literacy program didn't say I was too old. I decided that myself. Don't you think I'm too old to teach reading?

Oh my goodness. No one ever said I sounded like a 'cool grandma' before. How old are you? Twenty-eight is a good age. I had just gotten married and was pregnant with my daughter. Oh, sorry, my grandson says I'm a boring old fool when I reminisce like that. Really, you do find it interesting? I haven't thought of myself as interesting in a long time. Thank you.

Yes, I do think of my daughter and husband more during Christmas. I feel hungry all the time. But food doesn't help. I'm not fat, just eat more this time of year. I cry each night thinking about them. Would you like to hear a poem about my hunger? Really, you would? It's by Edna St. Vincent Millay (1969):

> My heart, being hungry, feeds on food
> The fat of heart despise.
> Beauty where beauty never stood,
> And sweet where no sweet lies
> I gather to my querulous need,
> Having a growing heart to feed.

That's just the first part, but it's my favorite poem. Thank you for enjoying it with me.

No, I don't get out much. I don't go to church anymore. All of my friends have died and even the minister has gone away. I don't know anyone there anymore.

Well, that's a good idea. They do have a lunch program everyday at noon at the church. Do you think I should call the minister first before I go?

That would be nice. I'll call the minister tomorrow.

No, I never heard of the senior citizen center. I live over by the park near Little Five Points. Gosh, that center must be close to me in Decatur. Oh, I feel kind of shy to call over there.

Are you certain it wouldn't be too much trouble? I'd love for you to call them and have the center staff telephone me. Maybe I could lead a poetry group. Oh, that's wonderful about the eye check-up visits at the center. You are really informed.

Yes, I do have trouble reading, as if the print has gotten smaller (but I think my eyes have gotten worse). And, to answer your question, I haven't gotten it checked. I'm not sure which doctor to go to. My eye doctor died.

You think I need to tell you more about how my son-in-law and grandson treat me? Well, my grandson calls me a 'stupid old lady,' and that hurts my feelings. My grandson once threatened to hurt me with a knife. Mostly, my son-in-law doesn't call or come around very much. And he doesn't answer my message I leave him for days. When I was sick with the flu, I almost ran out of food and he didn't answer my messages even though I said I was sick.

Well, I feel I should let you talk with others. But it's meant a lot to me having the opportunity to talk with you. Makes me feel like a 'cool grandma.' Thank you so much. When the senior center calls, I'm going to ask them if I can talk with the counselor you mentioned so I can discuss my sadness and talk about my husband and daughter. Thank you and happy holidays."

Chapter Seventeen

The Loneliness of Victimized Older Adults: Abuse and Intervention

IT has been estimated that 50.8 older persons per 1,000 experience neglect or abuse with 26.3 per 1,000 suffering from passive neglect, 11.2 per 1,000 experiencing verbal or emotional abuse, 10.5 per 1,000 exposed to intentional or severe neglect and 2.8 per 1,000 diagnosed as physically or severely physically abused (Poertner, 1986). These figures are based on a study estimating the incidence of abuse and neglect "by randomly selected communities from five strata of Illinois communities, identifying service providers and asking them to report on their experience with the problem" (Poertner, 1986, p. 14).

Physical abuse and neglect

Physical injuries to older adults have been defined as situations in which a "person is slapped, bruised, pushed, physically restrained" (Poertner, 1986, p. 7) or, in severe physical abuse, there is "abuse which leads to severe injury or death" (Poertner, 1986, p. 7). In passive neglect, the older adult is

> Unintentionally ignored, left alone, physically isolated, forgotten, signs of this include inattention to clothing, weight loss, access to telephone (Ibid, p. 7).

Moreover, active neglect is defined as

> Financial exploitation, withholding of needed medicine, food, clothing, heat, housing, social contact, assistance with daily functions (bath, toilet, etc.) (Ibid, p. 7).

Severe neglect is described as "Neglect which leads to severe injury or death" (Ibid, p. 7).

While Barbara Anne was not beaten, her grandson threatened to harm her with a knife. There was evidence of passive neglect during her initial call to the hotline and throughout follow-up calls (four) by hotline counselors prior to Christmas. It appeared that both her son-in-law and her grandson were aware of her worsening eyesight, but did nothing to assist her with this problem. In fact, her eyes were deteriorating to such an extent that driving was dangerous. The eye examination at the senior citizen center revealed glaucoma that, when untreated, can lead to blindness. Fortunately, it was controlled by medication. She also needed some major adjustments to her glasses for clearer vision, both for reading and for driving.

Her grandson's stealing her possessions to finance his drug purchases involved financial exploitation, a form of active neglect. This was confirmed by the grandson, who was visiting his grandmother during one call from a hotline counselor. The counselor spoke with the grandson, asking him what was happening. The grandson freely admitted that he was "using grandma's possessions to raise my level of consciousness with drugs, so why would an old lady need so many things anyway?"

Emotional abuse

"Verbal or emotional abuse" has been described as occurring when a

> Person is called names, treated like a child, frightened, humiliated, intimidated threatened (Ibid, p. 7).

This is an interesting listing of both verbal and emotional abuse together, as if one term does not include the other. I think it is an accurate differentiation that is rarely made- that verbal abuse alone does not comprehensively cover the entire area of emotional abuse. Rather, there are subtle forms of psychological torture, like clenching a fist with no accompanying words or reaching out to choke someone (without actually choking them) and these nonverbal forms of emotional abuse often have a powerful impact on the victim. For Barbara Anne, her grandson's threatening to "cut you good" with a knife was experienced as both terrifying and a betrayal.

During the telephone conversation with a hotline counselor, the grandson denied that he would physically harm his grandmother. Barbara Anne explained that, "He would only harm me under the influence of drugs. I think I would feel safer with a new lock on the door."

The telephone counselor recognized the fear that Barbara Anne was experiencing. The emotional abuse, including the grandson's belittling and threats toward Barbara Anne, resulted in trauma. Barbara Anne described feeling frightened, having nightmares, watching and listening for every little sound.

> Since the family's protective and containing functions have failed, the initial task is to reestablish physical and emotional safety (Krugman, 1987).

The counselor worked with Barbara Anne to explore safety issues and Barbara Anne decided to change the locks in her home. Emotional safety was considered and Barbara Anne decided to only allow her grandson to visit her at the same time as her assistant minister came on his weekly visits to her home. When the counselor had called the church, an assistant minister had called Barbara Anne and asked if he could make weekly visits. Barbara Anne had been delighted with this offer. As she became more involved in the church, Barbara Anne shared the situation with this assistant minister who both worked and lived nearby. He requested that she notify him to come over prior to any visit from her grandson. The grandson, Jeffry, was informed he'd have to call before visiting, since new locks had been put on Barbara Anne's doors.

On Christmas day, this new method was put into effect and Jeffry's visit was thereby supervised by the assistant minister. This plan resulted in an absence of stealing or emotional abuse by Jeffry. When the son-in-law didn't visit on Christmas Day, Barbara Anne called him and asked that he come by that night. This was the first such request she had made to him and was only able to do so with the encouragment of the counselor. She also called up and requested her own inclusion in the senior center's lunch program and activities on a daily basis.

Breaking the cycle of loneliness, fear of communication, clinging to a grandson who abused her, depression, hopelessness and grief, Barbara Anne- with the help of the telephone counselor- was able to rediscover her sense of self and reintegrate around her own strengths, interests and hobby (poetry). In addition, she began increasing her involvement in the church. Barbara Anne also volunteered to teach children in a literacy program. And she disattached from her grandson's abusive process with guidance and validation from the telephone counselor initially and later from a therapist who visited the senior center where Barbara Anne attended daily. Barbara Anne started therapy, working with the grief relating to her many losses, including the deaths of her husband and daughter. She terminated with her telephone counselor on Christmas day when all of these other support systems were in place.

Problems of identification

Elder abuse is difficult to identify, because "elder maltreatment encompasses a wide range of acts and conditions, which suggests that policy and practice require greater specification" (Hall, 1989, p. 191). Furthermore, it has been suggested that "the inclusive concept of maltreatment requires differential criteria to define its major dimensions" (Ibid, p. 191). Moreover, neglect has been described as "the most difficult category to differentiate" (Ibid, p. 192).

The problems with identification are crucial since there can be no effective intervention without proper recognition of elder abuse. Hall (1989) argued that

> Our society's reluctance to intervene in the domestic unit and the limited resources allocated to protective services suggest that only the most patently offensive occurences will receive attention (Hall, 1989, p.192).

Hall (1989) examined case studies to validate types of abuse and delineated 43 "maltreatment elements." Some of Barbara Anne's experiences are included, such as "Not caring for health or seeking medical care," "Others take the elder's resources," "Verbal aggression-not specific," and "Leave elder alone for long time, abandon" (Ibid, p. 197). These elements are described as occurring jointly: 69.4% of the cases contain two or more of these elements.

In spite of the difficulty in identifying elder abuse, it has been suggested that this is a responsibility shared by all health providers, rather than only adult protective service agencies (Phillips and Rempusheski, 1986). In a case like Barbara Anne's, a time-limited hotline (Loring and Wimberley, 1993) was the conduit through which she reached out for help. It would be valuable if churches would track older persons who drop out of involvement, like Barbara Anne who had been active in her church prior to the death of her daughter and husband.

This type of out-reach strategy is crucial in identifying elder abuse, because older adults tend to deny that the abuse has occurred or may refuse to report it for fear of abandonment or retaliation (Hudson, 1986). Other possible reasons for the lack of self-reporting include believing that the abuse is deserved, feeling hopelessness about the possibility of help, or experiencing shame in acknowledging such behavior in one's children (Ibid).

Thus, identifying elder abuse is all of our responsibility, including therapists to whom the aging individual might turn for help with grief or other-related problems. When evaluating older persons, it is crucial to do an over-all evaluation that checks for physical, sexual and/or emotional abuse.

Kosberg (1988) suggested that some characteristics make an individual especially vulnerable to experiencing elder abuse. These characteristics include being female, advanced age, dependence, being a problem drinker, intergenerational conflict, an older adult who internalizes blame and has excessive loyalty, stoicism, isolation, impairment and possible provocative behavior (such as overly-demanding adults). At the same time, Kosberg (1988) described a profile of high risk caregivers as including the following characteristics: A problem drinker, medication or drug abuser, senile dementia or confusion, mental or emotional illness, caregiving inexperience, economically troubled, abused as a child, unengaged outside the home, unsympathetic, lacking understanding, unrealistically expectant, economically dependent and hypercritical.

High risk family systems are depicted by Kosberg (1988) as containing a lack of family support, caregiver reluctance, overcrowding, isolation, marital conflict, economic pressures, intra-family problems, desire for institutionalization and disharmony in shared responsibility. These are helpful guidelines for the mental health provider and therapist in detecting elder abuse.

More subtle forms of emotional abuse often result in visible symptomatology, such as somatic problems, depression, withdrawn isolation, crying and other grief-related reactions, sleep and eating disturbances, despair and hopelessness. Questions by the therapist regarding relationship systems and emotional treatment yield information about emotional abuse.

Theoretical perspectives of elder abuse

Cicirelli (1986) based an attachment model of elder abuse on Bowlby's attachment theory, suggesting that attachment continues from early childhood throughout the entire life span. This attachment includes proximity-seeking, exploratory and protective behavioral systems (Bowlby, 1979). The child is faced with separation from a parent as adult independence is established, so that the child learns to experience closeness and parental contact on a symbolic level. The mechanism of identification serves to incorporate aspects of the parent's personality and allows the grieving child to symbolize the parent in this parent's absence. Thus, feelings of closeness and similarity to the parent are viewed as attachment later in adult life. Proximity-seeking behavior continues to be an indication of attachment to a parent, even as the child- herself- becomes an adult. While the attachment theory is relevant to all ages, it is particularly poignant in respect to aging persons who are experiencing multiple losses.

Cicirelli (1986) suggests that a relationship exists between attachment, a form of bonding to one's parent and subsequent helping behavior on the part of the child/adult/caregiver of the aging person. If, for example, an adult is not well-bonded to an aging parent, yet is placed in a position of care-taking, this may set the stage for elder abuse. On the other hand, a closely attached adult child can often weather conflicts with an aging parent without abuse and with conflict resolution.

This is an interesting theoretical perspective in which an intervention base is suggested by the core of the theory. That is, strengthening the bonds between the abused older person and her caretaking adult child would be perceived as decreasing the threat of abuse.

The "situational model" is described as having popular support among clinicians, because it lends itself to an intervention framework in relationship to stress (Phillips, 1986). That is, as stress increases for the abuser, the probability of abuse toward the vulnerable victim increases. The victim is perceived by the abuser as being associated with the stress. For example, if an aging adult experiences poor health, this theory suggests that caregiving and/or other aspects of the illness may be experienced as stressful for the abuser. It has been suggested that "stress is intrinsic to prolonged caregiving" (Ansello, King and Taler, 1986, p. 320). Research on the impact of external stress on elder abuse is not conclusive and further studies are underway.

Phillips (Ibid) traces the types of research and theoretical support for this perspective, suggesting that the model has been proposed as an effective explanation for elder abuse due, in part, to its effectiveness in explaining child and spouse abuse which have been compared to elder abuse. There has been difficulty finding consistent research data to support this theory. The lack of support has been attributed to a number of factors, including the lack of comparison groups and representative samples in the studies (Phillips, 1986).

A somewhat different perspective of viewing elder abuse involves a focus on the intensity and density of abuse (Johnson, 1986) and this can be helpful to therapists. Intensity includes the frequency of abusive occurrences and the severity of these events, while density derives from the numbers of types of abuse identified in a single case. That is, in one case, physical, psychological, sociological and legal mistreatment can occur concurrently. Physical mistreatment is defined as including medical health maltreatment, bodily impairment and bodily assaults. Furthermore, psychological maltreatment includes humiliation, harassment and manipulation. In addition, sociological mistreatment involves isolation, role confusion and lifestyle incompatibility. Moreover, legal maltreatment is defined as material exploitation, personal exploitation and theft. This definition of abuse is based on extrinsic behavior manifestations (measurable observable events).

Yet another orientation for defining elder abuse is based on a needs-oriented definition developed by O'Malley (T. O'Malley, 1983). The environmental press model involves defining elder abuse in terms of the fit of the aging adult with her or his environment (Ansello, King and Taler, 1986). So that abuse would be defined (and intervention designed) in terms of the possible lack of competence in the older adult and/or the caregiver(s). Furthermore, the environmental press may be defined in terms of abuse of the victim, in which case this press should be reduced by separating the victim and abuser to provide protection to the older adult.

On the other hand, the environmental press could be defined as lacking if the victim was isolated, as in Barbara Anne's case. Thus, increasing the press by referrals to community resources would be an important intervention. Further research is needed in this area of identifying elder emotional and physical abuse, described as an invisible problem (Kosberg, 1988).

Exchange theory has been used to explain elder abuse by suggesting that abused older adults have less power and are less able to reciprocate with instrumental services than during their earlier lives: This results in a vulnerability among older adults who may be abused by more powerful adult children. These adult children may be extending instrumental services to them (J.J. Dowd, 1975). Older adults are viewed as having lost much of their power and have fewer rewards to share with others. In addition, caregivers, according to this model, have less to lose when abusing an older adult who is powerless and dependent. This model involves the weighing of rewards and punishments as a process of exchange during which individuals attempt to maximize rewards and minimize punishments during their interactions. Barbara Anne perceived herself as having less to offer as she grew older and her grandson voiced a similar perception.

On the other hand, Pillemer (1986) has argued that the abuser may be more dependent on the older adult, perpetrating abuse because of feelings of powerlessness and harming the aging adult to compensate for the lack of control over resources. This view would still fit the exchange theory from a different focus regarding who is the more powerless individual.

Another perspective involves the application of symbolic interactionism. The meaning that is given to actions is the crucial component of this theory, so that abusive caregivers "tended to ascribe negative motives and characteristics to the elders for whom they cared ..." (Phillips, 1986, p. 210). In abusive families, "negative characteristics and ulterior motives were ascribed to the elder's behavior and elders were viewed as "willfully difficult or uncooperative" (Ibid, p. 210). Thus, the meaning attributed to the older adult's behavior appeared to make the difference between abusive and nonabusive responses by a caregiver.

In addition, a social learning model has been used to explain elder abuse (Steinmetz, 1978). When children are abused, they may learn the type of conflict resolution that involves violence. Subsequently, if these children become caregivers to their aging parents, the learned abusive behavior becomes an interactive style with their own parents.

No one of these perspectives completely explains elder abuse. Each helps to understand the dynamics of harm inflicted on older adults by those who are family members, friends, or other caregivers. Others treat elder abuse between spouses as an extension of spousal or partner abuse among younger partners (Walker, 1984; Loring, 1994). Further research is needed to examine the validity of these theories and expand intervention programs based on them.

Epilogue

Hopes and Strategies for the Future

On caring

> In caring for another person I encourage him, I inspire him to have the courage to be himself. My trust in him encourages him to trust himself and to be worthy of the trust. Perhaps few things are more encouraging to another than to realize that his growth evokes admiration, a spontaneous delight or joy, in the one who cares for him. He experiences my admiration as assuring him that he is not alone and that I am really for him. His awareness of my delight in his efforts to grow has a way of recalling him to himself ... (Mayeroff, 1971, p. 44)

The emotional abuse victim journeys forth with a caring therapist into a world of new internal and external experiences. The survivor transforms her trauma from self-diminishment, self-loss, and self-destruction into an integrated and meaningful self-system and empathic, validating connections with others. This survivor identifies and recognizes the killing power of emotional abuse- both that which wounds her from without and the internalized self-blame and self-destructiveness:

It is a dead heart.
It is inside of me ...
It died on the word EVIL.
I did it with my tongue.
The tongue, the Chinese say,
is like a sharp knife:
it kills without drawing blood (Sexton, 1975, p. 36–37).

A unique challenge for therapists- diagnosing and effectively intervening in and treating emotional abuse. It seems amazing for such a powerful process to receive little recognition as operating alone, independent from physical abuse. Walker (1984) has suggested that emotional abuse- or 'psychological abuse' as she names it- is difficult to quantifiably measure, "even though the women's reports were that it caused them the most pain" (p. 27).

For Jen, her healing in therapy was a transformation from suicidal ideation to a fulfilling, integrated life. Connections with empathic others was a crucial aspect of her well-being as it is for others (Jordan *et al.*, 1991). Reconnecting with the community and with issues in which she believed were essential aspects of her healing and growth. This is another aspect of recovery for trauma survivors (Herman, 1992).

Janet was sentenced in federal court to five years probation with family violence counseling mandated. Wendi accepted a plea bargain and was incarcerated for six months, after which she stayed in a transition house (for another six months) working in the community during the days and incarcerated in the building each evening. Following twelve months, she was released on probation with mandated counseling in the area of family violence.

Jeremy continues his interest in acting and writing. After completing high school, he went to a college with an outstanding drama department. Jeremy is studying acting and the theater.

Barbara Anne has developed a year-round hotline for lonely older adults. She keeps in touch with mental health professionals who make referrals and guide her. She also volunteers with a community agency where she helps young pregnant teenagers.

Barbara Anne initiated a poetry group at the senior center, purchased new glasses, limits her grandson's visits to supervised time with the assistant minister present, and is active in her church. In addition, she is in therapy to deal with her grief regarding the loss of her daughter and husband. She volunteered to serve on the holiday hotline which she originally called for help, herself, during its operation the next Christmas/Channuka.

There must be a larger, social recognition of emotional abuse as an independent, insidious process that damages children and adults. Greater awareness is needed concerning the tremendous and tragic power of emotional abuse which can be the antecedent to murder. It would be valuable if our laws could be extended to forbid emotional torture and stalking, as well as physical battering and stalking. Fortunately, physically stalking another has become a punishable offense in some states.

Stalking in emotional abuse can include threats to harm and pursuit/harm/damage to the victim's pets, family (children, sisters, brothers, parents), and possessions. The stalking often involves following the victim around the house with continued threats, or continuous threatening and jealous telephone calls to the victim at work or a relative's house. In one case, the abuse victim refused to speak with the abuser. This abuser kidnapped the victim's child (his stepchild), placed the child in his car, drove to the front of the victim's house, and informed the victim at her front door that she would speak to him or the child sitting out in the car (and he pointed this out to the terrified victim) would be killed. Other common threats involving children include threats to rape or burn. Moreover, broken, ripped, burned, and otherwise destroyed property can be a wrenching experience for an emotionally abused child. Harming pets (especially dogs) is not uncommon in cases where emotional abuse is severe. Witnessing the punching of dogs, slamming them against walls, and/or beating them with such an object as a hammer is a devastating emotionally abusive experience for a child or adult.

Trauma is a real consideration for therapists, themselves, when they are engaged in absorbing information regarding harm to women, children, pets, and/or property as forms of emotional abuse. Traumatized therapists may recognize somatic problems in themselves, as well as such characteristic trauma symptoms as sleeping/eating problems, flashbacks, and intrusive thoughts. After hearing about emotional abuse involving harm to animals, children, and terrible cruelty, I feel queasy, like I'm riding on a rough airplane flight. I think it's a metaphor for the truth that severe violence makes me sick. I do not drive a car until after having time to talk with a colleague or self-sooth in some constructive manner (like reading a mystery book for a few minutes).

If the therapist is involved in a high-profile case, television and radio journalists may try to elicit information immediately following a trial or incident. Therapists and intervention specialists should be alert to ethics in the area of sharing confidential information. Even after a court case has been completed, recorded, and a transcript is available, the therapist should be aware of confidential information unavailable to the general public. Many therapists in the community are not aware that their records can be suppoened for court involving family violence cases. All incidents of family violence and various types of abuse should be noted in records. Language depicting the victim in records should be accurate. And therapists need to be alert to personal safety issues while working in the area of family violence.

Thus, therapists should be aware of their own emotions, internal and external safety, trauma, and the health and well-being of the victim. For emotionally abused individuals, healing lies in the identification of the abuse process and the journey through painful awareness, exciting validation, holistic reintegration, and rebirth of self-hood. The guide in healing is the therapist who "strives to be reliable, attentive, empathic, and sympathetically responsive, and also to encourage ..." (Bowlby, 1988, p. 152). The therapist is a "companion for his patient in the latter's exploration of himself and his experiences" (Bowlby, 1988, p. 151). The therapist is a champion of the victim's self.

Ultimately, a victim can transform her sense of self from the disintegrating and despairing trauma of emotional abuse into the integrating hopefulness of a surviving human. Vulnerable and cautious, the survivor strives to maintain an integration and recognize when further abuse threatens her newly developed coping mechanisms. Reintegration is a skill the survivor will use repeatedly as emotional abuse is identified and as she protects herself. She is never finished- surviving for always. Jen gained an awareness of her ongoing vulnerability:

> Even now that I feel so much more whole and safe, I have to be careful. It's like the old anxious attachment ways can re-surface. Usually they revisit during some kind of abandoning or abusive experience. It's useful to think of my vulnerability as chronic. I need periodic check-ups and attention to the resurgence of symptoms. Then I don't find myself down the hole of abuse with no way back out. It's comforting to know that I can request a 'therapeutic debriefing' if trauma gets me down.

Learning new attachment patterns with oneself and with others is one of the most exciting aspects of healing from emotional abuse. To the extent that emotionally abusive individuals can be helped and guided in changing their behavior, the responsibility for stopping violence is placed in their hands- those who use control and power to diminish the humanity of another.

At the same time, the emotional abuse survivor is not dependent on external change for safety or healing. Her sense of safety grows

1) from her enhanced ability to identify and disattach from the emotional abuse process,
2) by disattaching from her own traumatic reactions while integrating the trauma,
3) through rediscovering and reconnecting with her sense of self,
4) in the creation and connection with her own craft and dream,
5) as a part of newly formed connections with others in community,
6) when her disattachment allows her to leave severe external emotional abuse and, when appropriate, obtain legal protection.

Thus, social and emotional levels of safety and care are developed by the survivor, while- at the same time- her well-being is looked after by others who care about her and by herself.

> The essence of trauma is that a person's sense of safety in the world is seriously compromised. The provision of a safe environment is the most important aspect of the treatment of victims of trauma. The sense of safety must encompass physical, emotional, social, and moral levels of care (Bloom, 1994, p. 479).

Readers of this book are urged to be aware of any of their own traumatic reactions while reading about these issues. Headaches, generalized fear and/or sadness, difficulty sleeping, poor appetite, and/or problems concentrating- all of these and more would be normal reactions to reading about such trauma and sadness.

Among emotional abuse survivors, the reconnection with self and others is ongoing, dramatic, and hopeful. Transformation restores the humanity once diminished by emotional assault.

References

American Medical Association. (1992) Diagnostic and treatment guidelines on domestic violence. Chicago, IL: American Medical Association.

American Psychiatric Association: Diagnostic and Statistical Manual of Mental Disorders, Fourth Edition. Washington D.C., American Psychiatric Association, 1994.

Ansello, E.F., King, N.R. and Taler, G. (1986) The environmental press model: A theoretical framework for intervention in elder abuse. In K.A. Pillemer, and R.S. Wolf (Eds.), *Elder abuse: Conflict in the family* (pp. 314–330). Dover, MA: Auburn House Publishing Company.

Blank, A.S. (1985) The unconscious flashback to the war in vietnam veterans: Clinical mystery, legal defense, and community problem. In S.A. Sonnenberg, A.S. Blank, and J.A. Talbot (Eds.), *The trauma of war: Stress and recovery in vietnam veterans* (pp. 295–308). Washington D.C.: American Psychiatric Press, Inc.

Bloom, S.L. (1994) The sanctuary model: Developing generic inpatient programs for the treatment of psychological trauma. In Williams and Sommer (Eds.), *Handbook of Post-traumatic Therapy*. (474–491). Westport, CT: Greenwood Press.

Bloom, S.L. (1995) The sanctuary model: A short-term hospital approach to the treatment of chronic PTSD. (1–31). In C. Figley and R. Kleber (Eds.), *Beyond trauma*. New York: Plenum Publishing Corp.

Bohn, D.K. (1990) Domestic violence and pregnancy. *Journal of Nurse-Midwifery*, 35, 86–98.

Borkowski, M., Murch, M. and Walker, V. (1983) *Marital violence: The community response.* London: Tavistock Publications.

Bowlby, J. (1973) *Attachment and loss volume II: Separation anxiety and anger.* New York: Basic Books, Inc., Publishers.

Bowlby, J. (1979) *The making and breaking of affectional bonds.* New York: Tavistock/Routledge.

Bowlby, J. (1988) *A secure base.* New York: Basic Books, Inc., Publishers.

Browne, A. (1987) *When battered women kill.* New York: The Free Press, A Division of Macmillan, Inc..

Cicirelli, V.G. (1986) The helping relationship and family neglect in later life. In K.A. Pillemer and R.S. Wolf (Eds.), *Elder abuse: Conflict in the family* (pp. 49–66). Dover, MA: Auburn House Publishing Company.

Courtois, C.A. (1988) *Healing the incest wound.* New York: W.W. Norton and Company.

Douglas, M.A. (1987) The battered woman syndrome. In D.J. Sonkin (Ed.), *Domestic violence on trial: Psychological and legal dimensions of family violence* (pp. 39–54). New York: Springer Publishing.

Dowd, J.J. (1975) Aging as social exchange: A preface to theory. *Journal of Gerontology*, 31, 584–595.

Dunford, F.W., Huizinga, D., and Elliott, D.S. (1990) The role of arrest in domestic assault: The omaha police experiment. *Criminology*, 28, 183–206.

Dutton, D. and Painter, S.L. (1981) Traumatic bonding: The development of emotional attachments in battered women and other relationships of intermittent abuse. *Victimology: An International Journal*, 6, 139–155.

Ewing, C.P. (1987) *Battered women who kill: Psychological self-defense as legal justification.* Lexington, MA: Lexington Books.

Ferraro, K.J. (1979) Physical and emotional battering: Aspects of managing hurt. *California Sociologist*, 2, 134–149.

Follingstad, D.R. and Neckerman, A.P. (1988) Reactions to victimization and coping strategies of battered women: The ties that bind. *Clinical Psychology*, 8, 373–390.

Follingstad, D.R., Rutledge, L.L., Berg, B.J., Hause, E.S. and Polek, D.S. (1990). The role of emotional abuse in physically abusive relationships. *Journal of Family Violence*, 5, 107–120.

Fortune, M.M. (1987) *Keeping the faith.* New York: Harper San Francisco a division of Harper Collins Publishers.

Fortune, M.M. (1991) *Violence in the family.* Cleveland: The Pilgrim Press.

Garbarino, J., Guttmann, E. and Seeley, J.W. (1989) *The psychologically battered child.* San Francisco: Jossey-Bass Publishers.

Gondolf, E.W. (1985) Anger and oppression in men who batter: Empiricist and feminist perspectives and their implications for research. *Victimology: An international Journal*, 10, 311–324.

Graham,-Dee-L.R., Rawlings, E. and Rimini, N. (1988) Survivors of terror: Battered women, hostages, and the stockholm syndrome. In K. Yllo, and M. Bograd (Eds.), *Feminist perspectives on wife abuse* (pp. 217–233). Newberry Park, CA: Sage Publications, Inc.

Hall, P.A. (1989) Elder maltreatment items, subgroups, and types: Policy and practice implications. *International Journal of Aging and Human Development*, 28, 191–205.

Hammond, N. (1989) Lesbian vicitms of relationship violence. *Women and Therapy*, 8, 89–105.

Hearst, P. and Moscow, A. (1982) *Every secret thing*. New York: Doubleday.

Herman, J.L. (1992) *Trauma and recovery*. USA: Basic Books.

Hilberman, E. and Munson, K. (1977–78) Sixty battered women. *Victimology: An International Journal*, 2, 460–467.

Hofeller, K.H. (1982) *Social, psychological, and situational factors in wife abuse*. CA: R and E Research Associates.

Hops, H. (1982) Social–skills training for socially withdrawn/isolate children. In P. Karoly and J.J. Stefren (Eds.), *Improving children's competence: Advances in child behavioral analysis and therapy*. Volume 1. Lexington, MA: Lexington Books.

Hudson, M.F. (1986) Elder mistreatment: Current research. In K.A. Pillemer and R.S. Wolf (Eds.), *Elder abuse: Conflict in the family*. Dover, MA: Auburn House Publishing Co.

Hudson, W.W. and McIntosh, S.R. (1981) The assessment of spouse abuse: Two quantifiable dimensions. *Journal of Marriage and the Family*, 43, 873–875.

Johnson, T. (1986) Critical issues in the definition of elder mistreatment. In K.A. Pillemer, and R.S. Wolf (Eds.), *Elder abuse: Conflict in the family*. (pp. 167–196). Dover, MA: Auburn House Publishing Company.

Jordan, J.V., Kaplan, A.G., Miller, J.B., Stiver, I.P. and Surrey, J.L. (1991) *Women's growth in connection*. New York: The Guilford Press.

Kohut, H. (1986) *The restoration of the self*. Madison, CT: International Universities Press, Inc.

Kosberg, J.I. (1988) Preventing elder abuse: Identification of high risk factors prior to placement decisions. *The Gerontologist*, 28, 43–50.

Krugman, S. (1987) Trauma in the family: Perspectives on the intergenerational transmission of violence. In B.A. van der Kolk (Ed.), *Psychological trauma*. (pp. 127–151). Washington D.C.: American Psychiatric Press, Inc.

Loring, M.T. and Smith, R.W. (1994) Health care barriers and interventions for battered women. *Public Health Reports*, 109, 328–338.

Loring, M. (1994) *Emotional Abuse*. Lexington, MA: Lexington Books.

Loring, M. and Wimberley, E.T. (1993) The time limited hotline. *Social Work*, 38, 344–346.

Martin, D. (1976) *Battered wives*. New York: Pocket books.

Mayeroff, M. (1971) *On caring*. New York: Harper and Row, Publishers.

McCleer, S.V. and Anwar, R. (1989) A study of battered women presenting in an emergency department. *American Journal of Public Health*, 79, 65–66.

Murphy, C.M. and O'Leary, K.D. (1989) Psychological aggression predicts physical aggression in early marriage *Journal of Consulting and Clinical Psychology*, 57, 579–582.

NiCarthy, G. (1986) *Getting free: A handbook for women in abusive relationships*. Seattle, WA: Seal Press.

Niles, D. (1992) Post trauma intervention strategies. – Part 1. *The Advocate*, 15, 11.

Ochberg, F.M. (1991) Post-Traumatic Therapy. *Psychotherapy*, 28, 5–15.

O'Malley, T., Everitt, D., O'Malley, H. and Campion, E. (1983) Identifying and preventing family mediated abuse and neglect of elderly persons. *Annals of Internal Medicine*, 98, 998–1005.

Partnoy, A. (1992) *Revenge of the apple*. San Francisco: Cleis Press, Inc.

Patrick-Hoffman, P. (1982) *Psychological abuse of women by spouses and live in lovers*. The Union For Experimenting Colleges and Universities: Unpublished doctoral dissertation.

Phillips, L.R. (1986) Theoretical explanations of elder abuse: Competing hypotheses and unresolved issues. In K.A. Pillemer, and R.S. Wolf (Eds.), *Elder abuse: Conflict in the family*. (pp. 197–217). Dover, MA: Auburn House Publishing Company.

Phillips, L.R. and Rempusheski, V.F. (1986) Making decisions about elder abuse. *Social Casework: The Journal of Contemporary Social Work*, 67, 131–140.

Pillemer, K.A. and Wolf, R.S. (1986) *Elder abuse: Conflict in the family*. Dover, MA: Auburn House Publishing Company.

Poertner, J. (1986) Estimating the incidence of abused older persons. *Journal of Gerontological Social Work*, 9, 3–15.

Porterfield, K.M. (1989) *Violent voices: 12 steps to freedom from verbal and emotional abuse*. Deerfield Beach, FL: Health Communications, Inc.

Rounsaville, B.J. (1978) Battered wives; Barriers to their identification and treatment. *American Journal of Orthopsychiatry*, 48, 487–494.

Russell, D.E. (1982) *Rape in marriage*. New York: Collier Books.

Seligman, M. (1975) *Helplessness.* San Francisco: W.H. Freeman and Company.

Sexton, A. (1975) *The awful turning toward god.* Boston: Houghton Mifflin Company.

Shainberg, D. (1983) *Healing in psychotherapy: The process of holistic change.* Philadelphia: Gordon and Breach Science Publishers.

Sherman, L.W., Schmidt, J.D., Rogan, D.P., Smith, D.A., Gartin, P.R., Cohn, E.G., Collins, D.J. and Bacich A.R. (1992) The variable effects of arrest on criminal careers: The milwaukee domestic violence experiment. *The Journal of Criminal Law and Criminology*, 83, 137–169.

St. Vincent Millay, E. (1969) *Collected Lyrics.* New York: Harper and Row, Publishers.

Steinmetz, S. (1977) *The cycle of violence: Assertive. aggressive, and abusive family interaction.* New York: Praeger.

Steinmetz, S.K. (1978) The politics of aging: Battered parents. *Society*, 15, (5), 54–55.

Stocking, S. and Arezzo, D. (1979) *Helping friendless children: A guide for teachers and parents.* Boys Town, NE: Boys Town Center for the Study of Youth Development.

Straus, M.A. (1974) Leveling, civility, and violence in the family. *Journal of Marriage and the Family*, 36, 13–29.

Straus, M.A., Gelles, R.J. and Steinmetz, S.K. (1988) *Behind closed doors: Violence in the American family.* Newbury Park, NJ: Sage Publications.

Symonds, M. (1975) Victims of violence: Psychological effects and aftereffects. *Journal of Psychoanalysis*, 35, 19–26.

Terr, L. (1990) *Too scared to cry.* New York: Basic Books.

Tilden, V.P. (1989) Response of the health care delivery system to battered women. *Issues in Mental Health Nursing*, 10, 309–320.

Tolman, R.M. (1989) The development of a measure of psychological maltreatment of women by their male partners. *Violence and Victimology*, 4, 159–172.

van der Kolk, B.A. (1987) *Psychological trauma.* Washington D.C.: American Psychiatric Press, Inc.

Walker, L.E. (1979) *The battered woman.* New York: Harper and Rowe.

Walker, L.E. (1983) Victimology and psychological perspectives of battered women. *Victimology: An International Journal*, 8, 82–104.

Walker, L.E. (1984) *The battered woman syndrome.* New York: Springer Publishing Company.

Warshaw, C. (1989) Limitations of the medical model in the care of battered women. *Gender and Society,* 3, 506–517.

Wiehe, V.R. and Herring, T. (1991) *Perilous rivalry: When siblings become abusive*. Lexington, MA: Lexington Books. Womankind Inc. (1992, November) Facts about family violence and hospitals. *Hospitals*, p. 25.

WomanKind Inc. (1992, Nov.). Facts about family violence and hospitals. *Hospitals*, 24–30.

Index